"Father Sturm was an inspiration to many of us growing up. Now, through his book, he will inspire many more!"

- *Tom Fontana, award winning writer and producer & former student.*

"I am pleased to grant your request for the Nihil Obstat and Imprimatur. Congratulations on your good work. I am sure your spiritual insights and reflections will provide enlightenment and spiritual growth to all who have the privilege and the opportunity to read your book."

- *Most Rev. Henry J. Mansell, Bishop of Buffalo, NY*

"*Life's a Dance, Not a Dress Rehearsal,* is Father John Sturm's love letter to his God and all those souls the legendary Buffalo area Jesuit encountered. This breathtaking collection of reflections and gentle, loving counsel is a practical primer on spirituality and an eminently sensible guidebook for salvation."

- *William O'Shaughnessy, Chairman Whitney Radio*

"Dear Father Sturm - Just a few words to express my gratitude for your spiritual guidance written in the weekly bulletin. They have been of ever increasing importance in my personal quest to find God in the tumult of life."

- *Roger Wittig, parishioner of St. Michael's Church*

"What a privilege it is to share the full and loving life of Father John G. Sturm, S.J. and the wisdom and excitement of his magnificent messages ... utilizing print, radio, television and website opportunities."

- *Jerry Flashner, LIVING PRIME TIME*

"When I first met John Sturm, I thought he had entered the Society of Jesus on an athletic scholarship. His book relates his spiritual awakening in such a simple, direct, unpretentious, and utterly honest style that it is not only appealing but compelling. I was personally delighted that the former Canisius speedster has not lost his wonderful sense of humor."

- *Vincent O'Keefe, S.J., Classmate of John Sturm, S.J.*

Father John,

the downtown priest says

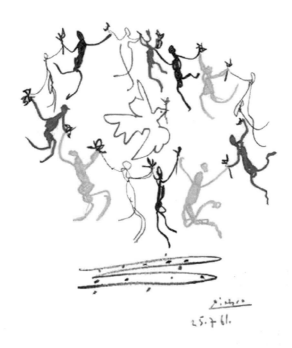

life's a dance,

not a dress rehearsal.

A book of spiritual awakening by Fr. John G. Sturm, S.J.

Dedication

This work is dedicated to the Sacred Heart of Jesus and all His Mercy. My heartfelt thanks to my parents, John and Catherine. A great voice of gratitude to my family.

There is a wealth of thanks in my heart to my Brothers in Christ and to my Jesuit education and the Society of Jesus.

I thank God for all my ministries as Prefect of Discipline, Marriage Encounter, Prayer Groups, St. Michael's Parish and all the people who have influenced me in many beautiful ways.

Many thanks to my many friends who encouraged me to write and aided me in this venture.

My appreciation to my sister, Sister Noreen, OSF, and Fr. James Ruddick, S.J. for special editing.

Fr. John's first blessing to his mother

Preface

I wrote this book for the greater honor and glory of God. We were all created in the image and likeness of God. We were created at the Hands of the Master Architect. We were given all the necessary means to enjoy the gift of life. God created us to be happy, but, for untold reasons, many are looking in the wrong direction.

Try to imagine this: God dances creation. You are the dance. He is the dancer. You cannot have a dance without the dancer. But, there can be the dancer without the dance. The dancer and the dance are intimately connected. You are intimately united with Almighty God. He dances in you in creation. You are His dance.

There is the old story of the fellow who lost his ring. He was looking and looking. Finally another person asked him if he could help. "Where did you lose the ring sir?" The old guy replied, " About three houses down there." "Why are you looking here?" The old guy said, "There is more light here."

That is exactly what is happening to our generation. The people are looking for happiness in all the wrong places. They do not recognize their own self worth, their own goodness. They really do not recognize that they are a gift to life. Consequently, they look all over to find peace and happiness, instead of within themselves.

I found the following story in a book of DeMello. There is the story of the chicken farm. An eagle egg was misplaced in a hen house. The eagle was born and lived with all the other chickens. It learned to cackle, flap its wings. It scratched for its food. One day the eagle looked up and saw this majestic bird floating lazily in the blue sky. He sighed and said, "I wish I was like that and could fly." The chicken next to him said, "You are only a chicken and will never fly like that." The eagle never knew who he was and remained a chicken.

Too often people live their lives as others show and tell them. They believe they are someone else and try to be someone else and never recognize their own self-worth.

This book tries to aid the reader in seeing his own beautiful self and how to appreciate his life and the life around him. Life can be beautiful and there are many neat parts for you.

God gave you this beautiful existence of human life. It is now your responsibility to discover your own beauty and how to share it with others.

Life is a dance. Dance the Dance. Do not sit on the sidelines. Life is not a dress rehearsal.

Read slowly. At the end of each section there is a question for your reflection. There is also space to answer it or to question it.

Make this book your friend. "The neat part is ahead."
God loves you and always forgives you.

Personal History

I have been ordained a Catholic Priest for over 50 years and have been extremely happy in my vocation. To live and work for the greater honor and glory of God is filled with countless built-in rewards.

When I began writing the bulletins for St. Michael's Church, I always ended by signing The Downtown Priest. The name just caught on and the people liked it. So did I. I was born in Buffalo and was baptized at St. Ann's church. The family moved to East Buffalo, Genesee and city line, in 1920. We all went to Most Holy Redeemer Church and School where I made my first confession and communion in first grade and graduated in1931. Grammar school was a joy for me. I was invited to be an altar boy. In eighth grade the team elected me to captain the baseball team. I then went to Canisius High School which was a tremendous experience. I was never the head of the class but I was captain of baseball and football. From there, I went to Canisius College on an athletic scholarship for football.

My next major question was, "What am I going to do with my life?"

In the summer time I had a job at Dold Slaughterhouse. Then the following years I worked during the summer at Dupont Cellophane Co. My decision to become a priest was not easy. I enjoyed life, the adulation from football. I had a job and delivered the Courier every morning at 6:00AM. I did not know what to do with my life.

I rode a bike to school every day and used to say "Hail Mary's" that I would not get hurt. I did not want to be laid up and not play sports. I went to church on Sundays and when I was not on the altar or in the choir I stood at the back of the church. One day the thought came to me that I should be a priest. Well, I fought that idea off. From time to time, especially if I was not busy, the thought came to me to be a priest. I was too interested in life, sports, job, and girls, that I did not desire that vocation. I played football at Canisius College in its great and glorious days of football. I worked at DuPont but as time went on I found that all of that was sort of boring. The idea of becoming a priest began to stay in my head as a song frequently keeps reoccurring. It was then I put the test up to the Lord.

I asked the Holy Spirit to guide me and said, "if I get hurt then that is a sign that I should become a priest." Well, the summer before I went to Canisius College I was in auto accident and could not play. But I told the Lord that I meant that I had to be hurt in a football game. You can really guess what happened. Before the season was completed, my knee was hurt and put me out. So being true to my word I said that now I have to become a priest. I told my parents after the school year. The reason I waited was I did not want the word to get out that I was joining the Jesuits. If the word got out it would spoil all the dates I had lined up for the summer. My parents were overjoyed and my Mother was filled with tears of joy. My Dad swelled with pride.

The occasion of telling my parents was another story. I had not reached 21, the legal age, so I needed my parent's permission to enter, which I thought was crazy. However it had to be done. I had not told them anything about my plans. In fact, I had not told or consulted with anyone. Thus, on a beautiful Saturday evening, I was sitting on the upper porch with my parents. In order for me to use the car, I had to have a good reason and be home by 12:00.

I did not have any reason so I told my parents for the first time that I was going to enter the Society of Jesus. I said, "May I use the car tonight I have a date." That is how it happened.

I entered the Society of Jesus in 1937 after two years at Canisius College. I taught at Regis High School in New York City for three years. I was ordained a priest at Woodstock College Maryland in 1950.

After ordination I was sent to Canisius High School as Prefect of Discipline. I was there 18 years and then retired and taught for two more years. I was moderator of the Mother's Club and the Father's Club for most of those years.

John Sturm, star halfback at Canisius College -1936

In 1971, Marriage Encounter was beginning and I became involved. I shared in that program with married couples for 20 years. In addition, I began the Engaged Encounter weekend for unmarried couples. I stayed with that program for fifteen years. This was in addition to the marriage encounter weekends.

In 1981, I volunteered to be an associate pastor at St. Michael's Church. I still reside there.

I am very active and involved with the theater group of downtown Buffalo. I attend prayer meetings. I have helped Lillian Bernas the stigmatist to receive an introduction to the Diocese of Buffalo. I enjoy playing golf. In addition, I spend a day per week with either one or two special handicapped teenagers. They have taught me a great deal about enjoying life with what you have. They have brought me great peace in how to accept life.

With all this background, teaching, dealing with others, retreats, and my own personal prayer, I began writing these articles. I hope you enjoy reading it. Share or buy a book for a friend.

–The Downtown Priest, Fr. John G. Sturm, SJ. A.M.D.G.

Contents

1. **Spirituality**

God has given you a mortal life and a spiritual life. Your mortal life is self-evident and common sense declares to you how you are to live. The spiritual life on the other hand is a sleeping giant. It has to be awakened and fed. Now as you begin to read keep your mind and heart open. In order to learn, it is necessary that you are willing to change some of your ideas. Otherwise, you will never learn anything new. Make no rash judgments as you read and pray.

Spirituality means to wake up to life, to this beautiful thing we call human existence. People are born asleep, live asleep, marry asleep, die asleep, and never live. They never appreciate their own personal beauty. They do not see themselves as God sees them.

What is the difference between a saint and an ordinary person? The saints know that God loves them and all is well, and they have a deep awareness of this beautiful and lovely thing we call human existence. They realize that they are not perfect, but they are aware that God sees them differently. They are beautiful in God's sight. Consequently, their actions are different because their ideas of God are different.

If you believe that you are missing something in your lives or wonder if this is all there is to life, then there is a need to change. It is like going in to have your oil changed. In order to feel closer to the Lord, you have to change and listen to the Holy Spirit trying to teach you. Your biggest mistake in life is underestimating the graciousness, forgiveness, mercy and compassion of God.

Jesus loved stories for He spoke in parables. Every story tells you something about yourself. You do not read the words, you read between the lines. What is the moral, the idea? What is this story trying to tell you? You listen for yourself and not your neighbor.

Sometime ago the following story was on Spanish television. A father knocks on his son's door and says, "Jaime wake up." Jaime answers, "I do not want to get up, papa." The father shouts, "get up, you have to go to school." Jaime says, "I don't want to go to school." "Why not?" asks his father "Three reasons" says Jaime" "First, because it is so dull; second, the kids tease me; third, I hate school." And the father says "Well I am going to give you three reasons why you must go to school. First, it is your duty. Second, you are 45 years old and third, you are the headmaster."

It is tough to wake up. It is nice and secure in bed. If you want to grow in spirituality, something must change. God's bounty is limited only by us. It is not hindered by past history, not by your parents, nor what you were fated to be by others, nor by what you do or have done. What counts is knowing what God desires you to do in His kingdom and asking for it. What is your call in life? You were all made for a specific reason. What each does with his or her life is up to that person. No one can take your place. No one can perform the task for you in the same manner. You are different. When you discover your own beauty, you will discover the peace of Christ. You yourself alone are responsible for your happiness. Your life cannot be blamed on anyone else. Life is totally in your hands. My business is to do my thing and to dance my dance. As the Arabs say, "The nature of the rain is the same, but it makes thorns grow in the marshes, and flowers in the garden." The love of God is like the scent of a rose. The rose does not care who smells it. The tree gives shade to anyone who takes shelter in it. The tree even gives shade to the one who cuts it down. It even protects from the sun, the person who chops up the tree. Jesus just loves you.

For your reflection: *What does spirituality mean to you? What do you think of the statement, that you cannot act any differently than your concepts of God?*

Fr. John with his Mother - Woodstock College, 1949

2. **Opening Up to Spirituality**

Downtown Buffalo is changing. Some buildings are being torn down. Others are being gutted. The city has been slowly dying and now it is beginning to get new life. Some people object to the changes and others see a new future. People hate changes; for instance, look at the opposition to visions of the new Peace Bridge, the building of a beautiful arch, the changes on the water front. If there were no changes there would be no growth, no future, no new visions. A pond which is not fed by fresh water grows stagnant. I am going to share with you the struggles that I had to face, after Vatican II, I did not want to wake up, change.

The same thing is true of the spiritual life. People do not want to change. This is the way it was and this is the way it is going to stay. It is amazing how often you repeat your ways of acting. You go to a restaurant and order the same food, shop in the same stores, drive the usual routes. Do a check on yourselves. Families move furniture around in the same room. There really is no change because the same furniture is still present. To change, it is necessary to get rid of something or all things and start over. Jesus said that, "No one sews a piece of unshrunken cloth on an old cloak." Lk 2-22.

Thomas Merton, the great spiritual writer says, "In order to grow in spirituality it is necessary to get rid of your old ideas and concepts and start over."

When it comes to spirituality, people are like robots. You say the same prayers every day, you sit in your usual pews, and you are irritated by how others act in church. Your idea of God never changes. For instance, look at the notion of God you had as a child. Is it any different in you today? Why not? Your spirituality should have opened your eyes and heart to a more mature relationship with God. St. Paul wrote, "When you were young I fed you milk. Now that you are older, you can eat solid food." Now, today, it is time to get a deeper understanding of God's love for you. To do this, change will have to take place. Life is short. The Holy Spirit is a special and unique gift of God to set you free, to feel His Love. To grow, to see how God loves you, you need to alter and change your ideas and attitudes.

Life gets boring when the same thing is repeated every day. Prayer can be boring. I was bored. Children, parents in their relationship, the same job every day, the same daily routines causes boredom. The same is true of the spiritual life. It can get boring. Prayers never seem to be answered, the life and energy gained from prayer are no longer present and you feel far away from God. It is as if He has abandoned you and dropped out of sight. This feeling and sensation are the Holy Spirit trying to awaken you to the "new." Ask yourself, why do you change the furniture around, or change the drapes? The same is true for your spirituality. There comes a time when you have to change, to grow. I had to face the same challenges as you. I did not desire to be left behind.

⊕ **For your reflection:** *How do you meet change?*
*Recall the story of the young man who had everything and asked Jesus "What more can I do?" The young man went away sadly, because he would have had to give up something.

3. Way to Grow

The Scribes and the Pharisees were good religious people. Jesus came and preached the good news. They called Him a blasphemer and crucified Him. They did this, not because Jesus was a bad person, but because He was preaching something new, the good news. It was a threat to their basic beliefs. They would have to change.

To grow, it is first necessary to admit that you need to change. Then and then only will changes take place in your lives. New ideas and concepts cannot operate if hindered by the old. People are like flowers in a pot. The growth of the flowers depends on the size of the pot. Flowers can only grow so much because there isn't any room for the roots to spread. It becomes root bound. Then, it is necessary to replant in a larger pot. Spirituality is the same. For it to grow, something has to change. Even Jesus had to grow in wisdom, age and grace.

It is a gift to recognize the beauty of being human. You are created in the image and likeness of God. It does not make any difference whether you are yellow, black, white. You are all created in the same way by the best Architect in all of creation. Life is given to you to appreciate all that you are. You are a miraculous mixture of the best of everything. What has happened in your life is the result of your decisions. It is not the fault of God. Poor God gets blamed for everything.

People of all types have faith in God. They believe in something or someone. The difference in people is their beliefs and practices of praying. Religion or spirituality is the way each person prays, acts, and loves their neighbor, to put into practice, their faith in God. There is a difference between faith and religion. Faith is belief in God. Religion is the way you put your faith into practice. Everyone is basically a good person loved by God. Everyone is a child of God.

If a person wishes to grow in spirituality and get closer to God and feel a more intimate relationship with Jesus, change has to take place. No one is going to change you. Only you can change yourself. You may read all the prayers, read good books, listen to sermons, go on retreats and none of these will effect a change unless you are willing to be changed. It is up to each person. Two things are necessary. One: to admit that you are wrong and two: a willingness to change.

I used to act and pray the same way. When Vatican II was approved with all those changes, I was not going to change. I enjoyed the English liturgy but I took exception to many different things. I was not going to concelebrate and argued constantly against it at that time, I lived at Canisius High School. They had a concelebrated Mass, but I did not go near the sacristy. After one year all those priests were still priests and appeared very happy. So one day, I had to admit I was wrong, and asked them if I could participate. They gave me a hard time, in good humor. What a difference! The interior struggle to admit that I was wrong or mistaken was not easy. It took prayer and soul searching. I regretted that I had not changed earlier.

Once I admitted that I was wrong, the Good Lord could do something for me. For instance, I never made a directed retreat. This is a retreat where one person directs your prayer all eight days. Each day it is necessary to give a report of the prayer experience. I was never ready to submit to such scrutiny. Now I made up my mind to try a directed retreat. This led to deeper prayer and ultimately to beginning the Marriage Encounter Program and the Engaged Encounter for the Diocese of Buffalo. Later on I joined prayer groups. These things and the retreat I would have shunned if I had not changed.

You do not have to enter those programs, but if you want to feel closer to the Lord, then you have to change and listen to Him in your own person. I cannot tell you what to do but I can set the scene and you pray and act it out. You alone are responsible.

⊕ **For your reflection:** *In what way or ways do I have to change my ideas? Am I willing to try?*

Fr. John - 14 months old

4. **Reawakening of the Spirit**

When you claim that you are satisfied with God, or say things are good and life is fine, you put limits on Gods love. You are actually saying that He cannot give you any more gifts. When you read anything or hear anything, do not look at it with one perspective. Do not prejudge. Be open to the entire package. If you look through a pile of mail for a particular card, you may miss many beautiful things in your search. No one can be taught anything, who is not willing to listen and learn. This is the basic requirement to advance in the love and closeness to the Lord. Without this desire, the spiritual life of any person remains stagnant and does not get out of the groove. Life becomes boring. You are always the same. You are like a beautiful flower made out of silk.

You know from life that jobs, marriage, hobbies can become boring. Then it is necessary to sit back and ask yourself, is this all there is to life? There must be more to it. The same thing is true about the spiritual life. It may not appear boring but it is like a record that has a bad groove and the needle gets stuck. There is nothing new. Did it ever occur to you that God has more in store for you than you ever imagined? You are still being molded in His loving hands. Why do you limit your own beauty when God can make you more beautiful and loving? You constantly give good things to your children to make them happy. Why do you think God will not do the same?

When you are awakened to this reality, you are beginning a journey which will be more exciting than you ever dreamed or imagined. How do I know? It happened to me. It is still happening. I am learning every day. God has more work and challenges for me.

In the former chapters I have tried to share with you that change has to take place, to grow closer and more intimate with the Lord. Let us take a look at how you may have approached life. What are your attitudes, ideas, thoughts, hatreds, prejudices, lack of forgiveness, past hurts, concepts of God? Something or some things have to be eliminated in order to receive new life. St. Thomas Aquinas, the great theologian, said, "Our ideas of God are more wrong than right." It is necessary to rethink your ideas of God. If not, you become a broken record which always says and sings the same thing. You cannot get out of the groove. So it happens in your prayer life. If you find yourself in the same quandary and always asking the same questions and repeating the same sins and always praying the same prayers and thinking that God has forgotten you, then it is time for a change.

Why do you desire to be so unhappy, so complacent and not at peace? You seem to deliberately live in anxiety and fear and scruples, or you do not know how to move beyond them. You are blinded by your own ideas. Jesus came to give you peace. It dwells within each person. You will feel the peace of Christ, if you get rid of all the negatives within you. Do not look for happiness anywhere outside of yourself. It cannot be experienced until you find it in yourself. You may not blame anyone else or anything else for your unhappiness.

The first step is the hardest. You have to admit that you were wrong or at least mistaken. However, pride, stubbornness, laziness and indifference conceal a new view of life. You would rather be unhappy and live in fear, anxiety, hurts and doubts. You

Fr. John - 14 months old

have not understood that you are made in the image and likeness of God and are holy temples of God. The Potter is continually molding His children. However, the children are stubborn and unintentionally resist the work of the Lord. It is not always easy to follow the Lord. The second step is a willingness to listen and to unlearn. Here is where faith steps in and a decision must be made. There needs to be a willingness to listen, learn and to change. If you listen with a stubbornness and prejudice not to change, you go against the Holy Spirit who teaches all truth. You resist the Potter who is forming you.

There is always room for growth. The Apostles had to change their beliefs, their way of life. Jesus asked them, "Can you take up your cross and follow Me?" Why should you be different? You are only a finite person and do not know all things. The Holy Spirit knows all truth. You have the attitude that the Lord has placed you here and that is it, and you cannot do anything about it. Perhaps the Lord had better plans for you? It would be quite humbling when you meet the Lord and He shows you what your life could have been like if you had listened and had courage to change. Never underestimate God.

✝ **For your reflection:** *Why am I afraid of God and hesitate to grow closer to Him?*

5. **Growth Steps**

There are two steps to growth: first, to admit that I was mistaken and secondly, am willing to listen. It was not easy for me to face them. It was a struggle and really a step out in faith and trust.

I had been ordained for twenty years. My spiritual life was ordinary. I was very set in my ways, to say the least. I was always doing the same things, and I was performing them in the same way. I became critical and judgmental. I did not like the feelings. My confessions were the same with little or no improvement. Vatican II seemed to be very liberal, and I was not. However, I did like the Mass in English and facing the people. Concelebrations were too far out. The sign of peace was another distraction. I resisted and refused to give in. I was timid about giving up the past.

Charismatic prayer appeared on the scene. My reaction was negative. It was another stumbling block. There were many invitations to join a prayer group, and I refused.

Marriage Encounter, a weekend for married couples was another new thing. A Jesuit priest from New York City introduced the program to the parents of Canisius High School students. It was a real struggle for him to begin the program. But it was a no-no for me. However, one weekend I felt sorry for him and asked him if he needed help. He was frequently asking for volunteers and to feel less guilty, I volunteered. He gladly accepted my offer and drove me to the Grace Retreat House in Alden. As the weekend began, my initial reaction was negative, and I would have gone home except I did not have transportation. Looking back, I can see that God had something in store for me.

While all of this was going on, I noticed that the couples and priests I met were very happy and enthusiastic and full of life. The couples loved each other and they loved God. I did not feel the freedom and the courage to express myself as they did in such a loving way. I became jealous and sort of lonely. I desired to feel that freedom. It then became apparent to me that I was missing something. There is more to the spiritual life than I imagined. Remember I had been ordained 20 years, had been on two thirty-day retreats in addition to a yearly eight-day retreat for all of those years. Still, something was missing in my spirituality.

My back was against the wall. In order to change, I had to admit that I had been mistaken about my attitudes and ideas. No one likes to admit that he or she is wrong. It was the same for me. However, my sense of adventure and competition drove me to change. If you want to read a good book about change, buy "WHO MOVED MY CHEESE?" In many ways I was just like any other person. People do not want to be happy or they do not know how to be happy in life. You never want to admit that you were wrong or mistaken. There is something in the nature of persons that resists change. People do not like to change. It is easier to be unhappy than to admit that there is another side to life. There is also a fear that you will lose your security in life, afraid you will lose your faith, a fear of losing God. You like to have your own way and set of ideas. You say this is the way I was taught and this is the way I will stay. Why should I change now? I am satisfied with the way I am. There is a certain amount of satisfaction and joy in having your own way, rather than to admit that you may have been in error. This is nothing but another form of vanity. You see only one side of the coin of life. For many, peace, happiness, joy, no guilt, freedom, intimacies with God are like fantasies and are for saints. You do not realize that God can open up the hearts of anyone, if you have the courage to change. Is all of this a description of who you are? You cannot fool God. The same is true of the spiritual world as in the social world. The Scribes and Pharisees were good religious people but they did not want to change. They were in the forefront of condemning Jesus. You are a good person but what are you going to do?

The first step in change is to admit that you may be wrong. This is very difficult for everybody. People have changed in the past, so it is possible. I felt fear of being laughed at, ridiculed, fear of what God may do if I am wrong in taking this step, fear of change itself. I thought that this is for others and does not apply to me. I began to take a good look at my life. I have only one life. There are no retakes. Life is not a dress rehearsal. I never wanted to look back and say, "I wish I had that opportunity again." God gives His graces in many forms. God is all around you. Why waste time? My Mother used to say, "John, if you want to be happy in life you must seek it out yourself. Do not depend upon anyone else." The same is true of the spiritual life. If you want to grow, you have to take the chances and the risks. Look at the saints. That is how they lived and prayed. They knew that God loved them and that was all that was necessary. The opinion of others was not their problem. Jesus loved them. You alone are responsible for your life. You cannot put the blame on anyone else. You have to face the Lord alone. Remember that Jesus loves you and He has great plans for you. He, who has ears to hear, let him hear.

✠ **For your reflection:** *What do you think will happen in your spiritual life if you should change? What are you willing to sacrifice?*

6. **Unconditional Love**

God loves us unconditionally. It is the perfect love. There are no conditions on His part. God is Love. You love and live conditionally. I will be happy if you give me what I want, if I can have gifted children, if I had a better job, if I had better parents, if I lived in a better neighborhood, if the priest had listened to me, if the church did not change, and if my children would go to church, if we had two cars, if the mortgage was paid and so on and so on. Just look at all the unhappiness in the world and the lack of peace in a person and the discord in families. People can't imagine having happiness without their own things, a new car, a new job, being recognized for work, new house and other things. These are all conditions. If life, if a relationship is built on conditions, it is built on sand. Look at the divorce rate. If you want love and happiness, and enjoy the gift of life as God intended then something has to change. You would think that all the unhappiness and fears in the world would be enough proof that the ways of the world are not working. To rid your life of the above, give a serious thought to the following steps: first, admit you have been mistaken and second, be open to change.

Just look at the heartache, the loneliness, the fear, the confusion, the conflicts in the hearts of people and families. Suppose someone gave you a method to get rid of fears and guilt and all those negative ideas, would you have the courage and conviction to change? Would you have the courage and faith to step out? Look at the faith of Abraham when told to move his family to another place. He had no idea where or how. Faith is stepping into the dark and allowing God to lead you. The Disciples heard the call of Jesus and followed Jesus. They gave up their jobs, changed their way of thinking and were willing to listen to Jesus and to act. They did not have any model going before, except Jesus, to show them the way. They felt something different, so they changed and followed the Lord.

After much prayer and the edification of others, I made my first major step. It was not easy. Do not think because I was a priest that it was easy. My human nature is not any different then any other person. I went through the same ups and downs.

I was ordained twenty years when I had to face myself in the mirror of the changes taking place in the church. I realized my Mother trusted in God and just went along with all the changes. I had to give up my stubbornness about Vatican II. I had to admit that I was wrong about the Council. I was forced to reevaluate my life style, I had been taught earlier. I had to admit that I was mistaken about my ideas and concepts of God. I had to spend time in prayer over the statement that "we do not act any differently than our concepts of

God." It is really true. Try it. No one could take the first step for me. In faith and trust in God, and often with hesitant steps I was led along this new path of freedom and the love of God.

The first step was the most difficult, but with each step I gained more confidence in myself and in God. The only way you will know and experience God in a new way is to try the two steps. I know this from my own personal walk with the Lord. Life is short. It is necessary to convince yourself that you may have been mistaken about many ideas and concepts of God. Not easy. It is a miracle of grace to admit that you were wrong no matter the circumstances. You know the difficulty in saying to someone, "I am sorry." I felt the same. When I changed, life began to change. My first major step was to admit to our Jesuit Community that I was wrong about concelebrations. I had refused to join. Joining the group lifted a great burden from my spiritual life. Try to admit to your family gathering that you have been mistaken about them. Do this after giving them a hard time for many a month. It is not funny. Do it.

Then, I went to New York to be trained for Marriage Encounter. As I made the weekend, I discovered in myself a tremendous fear of sharing with married couples. For 20 years I had been dealing with young men and now I was supposed to share with married couples. I prayed over this for a long time, I really wanted to get involved. However, two fears were in my heart. First, I would be involved with married couples. The fear came over me, suppose I fell in love with one of the women, what would I do and how would I respond? Would I lose my vocation? I did not know. Priests in general are afraid of the intimate feeling of love. I was no different even though I had come from a very loving family. The second fear was, suppose someone falls in love with me. I did not know the answer. This stunned me. I prayed and reasoned, if God desired me to do this work then He had to give me the graces and to send the Guardian Angels. I would need all the help I can get. I stepped out in faith, as Abraham did. It was the turning point in my spirituality. I began to experience more and more the love of God.

✛ **For your reflection:** *Have you ever asked for more faith in following Christ? What steps did you take?*

7. **Hindrances to Growth**

My next venture: The charismatic movement had begun. I wanted no part of this. It was too demonstrative and outlandish. Several friends invited me to join but I refused in no uncertain terms. I finally gave in. I went to a charismatic prayer group in a Protestant Church. I did this with tongue in cheek. When invited to pray with them in their chapel, I went home. However, six months later I returned, for it was not fair to make a judgment on one visit. This time I joined in just to see what would happen. At first, I felt like a stranger in a foreign country. It took some time and then I became a regular member. All my friends could not believe the change within me. It takes a long time for me to learn.

Think about the two steps for growth and apply them to yourself and the circumstances in which you live. No one can do this for you, nor will the Lord. If you desire to experience the love of the Lord in your circumstances, you have to take the initiative. You will not find God in another's back yard if He is not in your yard first. If you see nothing wrong with your relationship to Jesus and are satisfied, you will never experience a deep and abiding intimacy with the Lord, you will never know the joy, the love and the peace and freedom that Jesus could have given you if you had asked. Do not make yourselves believe that what you have is all there is. That is the idea of the devil. God loves you and has more to share with you if you ask Him. Try it. You have nothing to lose and everything to gain. The sacrament of marriage is a very personal sharing sacrament with both partners joined in Christ. It is the gift of Jesus to the married couple to experience Christ in their loving relationship. God is present in relationship. Communication, sharing, acts of love, sacrificing for another, are ways of experiencing the love of Jesus in your hearts. Jesus is in your relationship.

Spirituality is like wearing sunglasses. I became accustomed to wearing them and one day entered a card shop. I thought it seems very dark in here, then I realized I was looking through dark glasses. I exchanged them for my regular glasses. The store took on new meaning. Spirituality is the same. You become so accustomed to one way of looking at things that you do not notice there may be another way. There really is a new world of God's love just waiting for you. Trust me. He has infinitely more ideas of life than you can imagine.

God is a lover. He desires to give peace and joy to His children. He enjoys surprising you. God never repeats Himself. God cannot be programmed. He cannot be tied down to time and place, cannot be made to follow a procedure, does not accept set ways, He does not like to tread the same path twice. God does not "come back," God simply "comes." On the other hand you repeat and try to program the Lord, to bribe Him by promises of prayers, sacrifices and giving up something difficult. These ideas are like sunglasses; they blur your eyes and you may not recognize Jesus when He comes. Look at the intellectual Pharisees and Scribes. With all of their false notions, they did not recognize Jesus. They crucified Him.

Willingness to listen to the "new" is in rhythm with the psalm "sing to the Lord a new song." This is the way to grow in the love of the Lord and give Him glory. You will have new life and a new vision.

Isaiah finally says, "Remember not the things of the past, the things of long ago remember not. See, now I AM DOING SOMETHING NEW. Now it springs forth, do you not perceive it? Happy the eyes which see the things what you see." Is. 43:18-19. All change must start first in yourself. There are five occasions in the New Testament where Jesus uttered the following directions, "You hypocrite, remove first the beam in your own eye and then you may be able to see the splinter in the eyes of your neighbor." Mt.7-5 In other words, change starts with you. This must become your firm conviction. This is a real step out in faith. The Lord will not force anything on you. The Lord invites you every day, personally. He sends a daily invitation. Recall how He invited many to the wedding feast, to be happy, to rejoice. All had excuses. What is your excuse? It will be very embarrassing to meet the Lord and find out all the things He desired and wished for you, if you had stepped out in faith.

Think and pray over the notion of change. Look at your own person. It is your relationship to the Lord. It is your responsibility. The Lord created you to be the one you desired to be. He has given you all the graces and gifts necessary to achieve it. You are not left an orphan. There is no need to depend upon someone else or something else for your happiness. True happiness is never found outside yourself. Happiness dwells within you. You may not blame anyone else for the way you respond to life. Your life is in your hands. God gave it to you.

⊕ **For your reflection:** *I do not act or believe any differently than my concepts of God. How does this affect me?*

8. **Hindrances to Growth II**

There are no short cuts in spirituality. Take up your cross daily. It is necessary to perform all the steps. It is a slow growth. Spirituality is not like reading a mystery story. You cannot go to the end in spirituality and say I've got it. You are familiar with the time Jesus asked His Disciples a very essential question, "Who do you say that I am." Mt. 16-15. How would you answer that question? Your answer dictates to you how you act and react to life. Did you realize that you do not act any differently than your concepts, ideas and images of Jesus? Can you define your basic ideas of God? Can you put them clearly in writing? You will see and then become aware, that your life style is dictated by your answer. You can only act in accordance with your ideas of God. This is important to realize, if you desire to have a more intimate relationship to God.

No one becomes a saint overnight except one who has been martyred. The growth in sanctity is like a tortoise. It is slow growth in the experience of God. For you need to be constantly aware of yourself and others as children of God. Behind all of this, is a ready and generous willingness to grow in God's Love. No one can approach God half heartedly. Jesus said "since you are lukewarm, neither hot nor cold, I will spit you out of my mouth" [From the book of Revelation] It is really all or nothing. This awareness creates within you a sensitivity to the needs of others. This love and awareness are the measure of your holiness. It is the way to show and manifest your love of each other and of God. Jesus said MT 25:40 And the king will say to them in reply, 'Amen, I say to you, whatever you did for one of these least brothers of mine, you did for me.' This is how to love one another and grow and experience the love of God.

Your mistaken attitudes and ideas and images direct and guide your entire lives. Anxiety, worry, scruples, any fear, fear of dying, loneliness and many other concepts hinder the growth in the love of God. These arise as a result of false images. You place hindrances in the way of feeling the peace and love of God. When you peel an orange, you take off the skin, when you peel an onion, you cut off layer by layer. In order to experience the love of God, it is necessary to eliminate all the mistaken notions and get down to the way the Lord created you. He did not create you with all your baggage. All the baggage was created by you. Since you dressed yourselves in that manner, you can rid yourself of it. It takes much effort and prayer.

Did you not know that you cannot love God more than you love your neighbor? Think about it. Jesus said, "whatsoever you do to the least of my brethren you do unto me." Just remember the story of the sheep and the goats. What you do for others, you do for the Lord. Your relationship to your neighbor is just like your relationship to God. When you love your neighbor, you are loving God. As you deal with others so you deal with the Lord. In the Our Father, you say, "Forgive us our trespasses as we forgive those who trespass against us." Again on another occasion, MT 5:23 Therefore, if you bring your gift to the altar, and there recall that your brother has anything against you, MT 5:24 leave your gift there at the altar, go first and be reconciled with your brother, and then come and offer your gift." Jesus said that you should "love one another as He loves you." There are no conditions. Experiencing the love of God starts with loving yourself as God made you and then reaching out to your neighbor and loving them and forgiving them. To make a judgment of another is vanity. Who gives you the right to judge another? Remember St. John said, "how can you say that you love God whom you cannot see and hate your neighbor whom you see."

Take a look at your prejudices. How do you act in the presence of minority? What are your thoughts when you see a white person with an African? We are a prejudiced people. We are brought up in a certain culture and have only one outlook on life. Nationalism is entirely against the commandment of God to love one another. No race or color is better than another. Boundary lines are man made, not God made. It is not only against the commandment, it is against common decency. Every country has lost lives in war and destruction. Look at the prejudices about various religions. Examine yourself and look at your reactions to life and situations in life. Prejudice is a cancer in religion. In order to grow and experience the love of God, it is necessary to get rid of all that baggage and begin again. If you want to grow in faith, then you need to step out and start all over. Let the Lord teach you and that is why He sent the Holy Spirit to teach you all truth. You have to grow in wisdom, age and grace. Being secure and feeling satisfied does not make you a close follower of Jesus. When you reach that state, one grows stagnant and stale. Look at a pond, which does not have flowing water. It becomes stagnant. Remember the story where the Master and the servant were working. The Master came home and sat down to eat. On the surface the story sounds selfish. The Master told his servant to fix me my dinner and when I am finished eating you may eat. The moral of the story is if you only do what is necessary you are an unworthy servant. It is the extra that counts and shows you care.

Read over and pray over the questions or the objections you formed. In the meantime, reflect on your own ideas. Can you describe basic notions of God, your ideas of Jesus? How do you look and perceive God in your daily actions? Do you see the connection between your acts and reactions and your ideas of God? It is necessary to realize this, if you desire to experience the love of Jesus.

I will give you an example of mistaken notions of God. If you perceive Jesus as a Judge how does this affect your actions? If you see Jesus as one who rewards, how does this affect your actions?   If you believe that God keeps records how does this affect your actions? Try it yourselves. Jesus came to set you free.

Michelangelo found a perfect piece of marble. He kept chipping away all that was not necessary. He ended up with the outstanding piece of art, the Pieta. When you let go of the baggage you will discover the beautiful way God made you. It takes time, but you are beautiful in God's sight. Now you have to believe it and discover it.

For your reflection: *If you desire to do something interesting, write the answers to the questions you have just read in this chapter.*

The Sturm family saloon

9. **Live in the Present**

To experience God, it is necessary to live in the present moment. That means your thoughts, feelings, attentions are all concentrated in the present moment. Listen to the following example.

Did you ever try peeling an orange for the sake of peeling an orange? If you peel the orange in order to eat it, you are not living in the present. The actions of peeling are in anticipation of the eating. Did you ever try washing dishes, just to wash dishes? If you wash dishes to get them clean, the mind is distracted and lives in the future. The saints understood this notion of God and lived it. Enjoy the present moment. God only exists in the present moment and not in the past and not in the future. You change with each minute of the day. God never changes.

How often have you wondered why you get so many distractions in prayer? Did you not foster this way of thinking? The mind does not enjoy silence. It does not enjoy being left alone. It constantly feeds on ideas and thoughts. You do two things at once. Consequently, in prayer it wanders. You work in the house and the music is blaring. You take a walk with earphones. You know all this from your own experiences. You do one thing and your mind is wandering or filled with worry.

Just reading these concepts may help you to analyze what is motivating your present actions. This awareness of yourself will help you grow in self- knowledge and lead you to a deeper love of God. Your prayer life will slowly change.

However, you will not experience God's love until you step out in faith and put into action what you have learned. It is one thing to know about football but you will never know the game until you have actually played and experienced the action. You will never know how to ride a bike by reading a book in the library. The only way you will know how to ride a bike, is to experience it in action.

Have you taken the time to see and understand your way of life? If you are secure and believe you are safe, you are the loser. God does not repeat, He does not go back, He is never cornered, He cannot be blocked in by prayer or your security. God is not stagnant. Love is not stagnant. It is dynamic. God desires to grant you graces beyond your wildest imagination. Just let Jesus love you as He desires, not the way you desire. Once you knock at His door, he will introduce you to a world beyond your wildest imagination. The scripture tells you so.

How do I know that all the above is true? It happened to me. I was very sure of myself before Vatican 11 erupted. When things began to change, I felt very uncomfortable, dissatisfied, stubborn, upset. I argued and would not try anything new. There was too much freedom. Confessions and Mass were not considered important. What did others know that I did not? How could they act that way and still remain good Catholics? On the other hand, many faithful joined prayer groups, sang in church and were not afraid to say that they loved God. I was outwardly stubborn but inwardly jealous. I had to confront myself and come to a solution. I could either change or become a cranky and complaining priest. Have you examined your life? People constantly admit that their confessions are the same, they commit the same sins, they do not seem to improve, complain that God does not answer their prayers, are filled with scruples, they complain about all the changes, they blame their parents, they blame anything but themselves. The list could go on and on.

I ask a child, "Do you know that Jesus loves you?" They immediately say, "Yes." I ask an adult, "Do you know that Jesus loves you?" They think for a minute and scratch their heads and say, "I hope so." Please tell me, what is the problem?

The New Testament is filled with the wisdom that Jesus loves you. He even said, "Just as the Father loves me, I love you." Where is your faith? How is it that you do not believe? Is it that you do not understand His love for you? In either case, something should be done about it. The decision is up to you. Why live in limbo? Can you endure the same hair style day after day? Is it not boring repeating the same action time and time again? Did the thought occur to you that you treat Jesus just as you look at your self or others? Isn't love life boring if you always love your spouse in the same way? People change everything in sight except their approach to God and their prayer life. Isn't that strange? How about Jesus? Why bore Him? Make a decision to change and grow in love.

Jesus loves surprises just as you like surprises. Jesus often surprises you. It is in this method of a surprise that you can frequently recognize Jesus in your life. It is one of the many ways Jesus can be felt and experienced.

The Holy Spirit is not dead. Jesus is not dead. God is not dead. What makes you think that there cannot be any changes in the church? Do you believe that God is finished with the world and has nothing more to offer? Do you think that God is finished with you? There is always the "new." Jesus said, "I have come to set you free." I bring you something "new." Where is your faith? "Oh ye of little faith," He exclaimed to His Disciples. Sports, put a limit on pay. God does not put a limit on you "Ask and you will receive." It is necessary to drop the old notions of God and come to the conclusion that Jesus loves you. This is leading a life of faith. Ask and ask again.

✦ **For your reflection:** *Why are you afraid to ask? Why are you afraid to grow?*

10. **Love of God**

What does the word "Love" mean to you? Write your answer. Try writing because when you put a pen to paper you will experience something new inside of you.

On another page write "I am a child of God." What does that statement mean to you? What is your portrait or image of God? Has it ever changed? Write it out. Moses, who was a personal friend of God, asked Him to share something of Himself. God gave him this revealing self-portrait "the Lord, the Lord God, gracious and merciful, long suffering, and abounding in goodness and truth" {Exodus 34-6} Is this your portrait of God?

Let me help you. If you had or have children, how did you manifest your love? How did you hold your infant child? Visualize how you watched them, fed them, forgave them, held no animosities, gave them gifts and loved them abundantly and so on. Why do you believe that you are any better than Jesus? You are a child of God. Jesus often called His Disciples "children." In order to experience more of the love of Jesus, you have to see yourself as a child of a very loving Father. Use your imagination. You are all children in the eyes of God. You really never grow up in the eyes and hearts of your parents. Jesus loves you the same way to a much greater degree.

Did you ever look at the way you live? You are trained to do two things at once. You eat breakfast and read the newspaper, you read a book and have soft music in the background, you drive a car and listen to the radio or tapes or use the cell phone. Youths try to study with the radio blasting; you jog or take a walk with ear phones. You live and deliberately do things to take your mind off of yourself. It almost seems necessary to keep the mind busy. It is scary to be silent and be alone. The mind is so used to being fed that it craves for action. Then you wonder why you get distractions in prayer. You have developed your mind to look for distractions. When you attempt to concentrate, and want to try to pray you are going against the way you have trained your mind. If you desire to eliminate distractions in prayer, then learn how to appreciate what you are doing each moment. Do one thing at a time. God lives in the present. Enjoy your own self and if you desire to grow in the experience of God's love, then change has to take place. You need to change your portrait of God. Then you cannot waver or look back. Jesus said, "Once you put your hand to the plow and look back, you are not worthy of the kingdom of heaven." If your portrait of God is stingy, callous, unmerciful, quick to anger or slow to bless, unforgiving, you are living in a cloud of error that has left you impoverished rather than blessed. Read Luke 9:20. "Then He said to them, "But who do you say that I am?"

God is love. Jesus loves His Father and He loves you with the same love. God loves you with an everlasting love. Use your imagination and faith and see God as a loving Father. If you did not have a loving Father, this may be very difficult to do. However, you have the gift of faith and just believe. Look at yourself and be aware of how you love God and your neighbor, your family. God and Jesus are better lovers by far.

Fr. James Dolan, S.J. wrote the following reflection on the Love of God. God is sending you a message of love.

"There is something unusual about this gift which I hope that you will notice. This day is your gift and there are no strings attached. It is a pure gift and you can use it as you see fit. I have "no ifs or buts." This day belongs to you. It is your gift from Me because I love you. There are no conditions on my part. You can accept the gift or waste it. Do not consider any right way of acting or any right way of living. I have no ulterior motive. I just want to love you. Any way you live, any way you think, any way you breathe, any ways you walk are fine with me. Any way you experience this day might seem very human to you but it is divine with Me.

Last night while you were sleeping, I was watching you and protecting you, I thought how beautiful you are. I began to reflect as I gazed on you whether you would please Me if you acted in a certain way today. I saw you as My gift of love and I clearly realized I have no particular desire or will for you. You do not have to guess My mind. I have no special plan for you. All I want to do is to love you and share My love in this gift of another day and to enjoy this day. I really love you. This is your day. Good morning."

⊕ **For your reflection:** *This is God's love letter to you every day. Everybody enjoys receiving a love letter. How does this make you feel? Remember that Jesus loves you.*

11. **Children of the King**

Please say at least two prayers every day. The first, when you wake up, give thanks and praise to God for another day. Secondly, when you retire, give thanks and praise to God for the events during the day.

Your faith tells you that you are all children of God. He looks upon you with love. Just look at the way you look with love upon your own children. Why should God be any different? When I observe parents with their little children, I see God acting in the same way.

Here are examples of what I mean. You yourself are an example. Remember how you looked at your first child for the first time? You have seen pictures of mothers holding their children close to them. You have seen mothers breast feeding their children. You have experienced men holding their own children and walking them to sleep. I remember my Mother and Dad getting up in the middle of the night because one of the three children was crying. I remember my Dad coming home from work to take my little sister to the Deaconess Hospital for appendicitis. In your life time recall the way you loved and disciplined your children. God is better at His job than you are at your job.

Now, please, take a look at God. If a parent can so love and admire her child, don't you believe that God holds you in His arms with great love and tenderness? Why Not? Is that parent better than God? Are you better than God?

Don't you think that it is a great sign of love and trust in a mother that she would allow someone else to hold her new born baby? God does the same for you in allowing you to hold His Son in your hands and receive Him in Holy Communion? You are children of God and He loves and trusts you. You are His hands and feet in this world. You are His heritage and the Kingdom belongs to you. You are children of a King. You belong to a Royal family.

Here is another parable or story or analogy. I have learned a great deal in spirituality by watching children and observing the love of parents.

A number of years ago I witnessed this scene. We were sitting in the kitchen and talking as the two-year-old baby was playing. The baby was opening the cupboard doors and pulling out the various kettles and so on. It seems to be a favorite pastime. The Mother let the baby go and never uttered a word or scolded the child or told her that she was naughty. When the youngster decided to change her routine, the Mother said, before we leave this game I will help you replace all those things. Of course, the Mother replaced most of them as the child imitated her mother. It happened every time I visited. Two years later. I noticed, when the youngster gets finished making a mess of the family room, the Mother says it is time to clean up and the child does it all by herself.

God treats you the same way. He never condemns you or criticizes, or judges you as bad. He gave you His Son as the Way to help you and clean up your lives. He aids you and helps you and listens to your prayers. He hopes, as you get older, you can do many things by yourselves and correct your mistakes. However, if you need help, all you need to do is to call upon Him. He is a loving parent. Jesus told you, "Ask anything in My Name and My Father will give it to you." Start to live by faith and trust in the word of the Lord. Enter into an exciting spiritual life. Memories can be detrimental or helpful in the spiritual life. If they are used as a basis for spirituality then they are detrimental. Memories are only memories they are not real. The incidents which caused them no longer exist. To grow in the love of God it is necessary to live in the present, in the present moment. Memories are things of the past. God is infinite. He does not repeat. Nothing is the same today as it was yesterday or the day before and so on. There are those who try to relive or recreate the past but it never is the same. You know this from your experiences of a vacation. You may return to the same vacation area, but things are never the same. The return vacation is entirely different. This is true in the spiritual life. A spiritual experience is never the same a second time.

The Scripture is filled with stories. Jesus loved to tell stories. A story is the shortest distance between human nature and God. You can learn much about how God loves you not only from the observance of the children but also from young men and adults. Remember the story of the young man who demanded the inheritance from his Father. The Father loved the boy and gave him the money. The boy ran away and spent all the money. As a result he was penniless and starving. He decided that he had made a mistake and was wrong. He determined to ask his Father's forgiveness. He changed his entire attitude and walked home. Even before the boy reached home, his Father saw him and the Father ran out to greet the son and give him a party. His brother got mad and would not celebrate.

Jesus does the same for all of you. All you need to do is two things, admit that you were wrong and secondly ask for forgiveness. This gives new life. The Father is more than willing to receive you back. Never think of yourself so unworthy or low or so sinful, that God could never love you. His mercy is infinite and everlasting. You may feel cheated in life but remember God did not make you that way. In His sight you are still a prince or a princess. He wants you to experience His lavish goodness which He has prepared for you. Do not underestimate the Goodness of God.

⊕ **For your reflection:** *Jesus told His disciples "When you see Me you see the Father." Another translation "When you see me, you see love." God is Love.*

12. **Reaching Out**

One of the things I did to grow in the love of the Lord was to reach out to my neighbor. I have a relative who has two disabled children. Thus, I became active with the Providence Community on Breckenridge. Sister Rose Mary Cauley is the Administrator. The sisters take in serious disabled children. I have attended the children's dances and have attended their Christmas party and picnic and Chinese auctions. This community needs help on various levels. I also joined a support group for parents of the special children.

For me, life is a gift. God has given you this gift so that you may experience how much He loves you and how He loves everyone. Consequently, to grow in the love of God, it is necessary to experience 'life'. The special children taught me a great deal about enjoying life with what they have. They are not worried about what they do not have. If you desire to see how to enjoy life, go to a dance with the disabled. It will take away much pain, anxiety, jealousy and poor self-image. When the music begins, they all take to the dance floor and dance. They do not care how they look or what you may think. They just enjoy dancing. That is exactly where God is. He is in the present moment, on the dance floor, enjoying life with His children. Life is a dance. You will drive home with a brand new experience of life and a deeper appreciation of the gifts you possess. Try it. When you grow in a deeper sense, of who you are and your gifts and your faults you will take a giant step in the love of yourself, God and prayer. Too often you lead your lives to please others and not have them think badly of you. You restrict your lifestyle because of peer pressure and consequently you are not free. God is not there. Why give others such power over you, so that you do not enjoy yourself? I live in such a way that if you enjoy my company, great, if you do not, that is your problem. As I say to people, if you do not agree, fine, if you do agree, fine. That is being free.

I had great parents who taught me about life. Too often you allow life to pass you by. You are bored, complain and get cranky. You have the notion that no one cares and no one bothers with you. The phone does not ring, very little Christmas mail or birthday mail, etc. There is no one to blame but yourself. You create life your own way. My parents taught me a great lesson: "John, if you want to enjoy life do not wait for it to happen. You make it happen." This is true even in the spiritual life. You are responsible for your spirituality. If you are bored with prayer or Mass, it is your fault. No one was created to make you happy.

From time to time, I offer help at the St. Luke's Mission of Mercy. This community is on Sycamore St. They offer help to the homeless and very needy. Their music ministry is admired by many. They can use many volunteers. Jesus gave the example. Go and do likewise.

Reaching out to another in many other areas is imitating Jesus, as He reached out to the sick, the dying, the lepers, prostitutes and the hungry. Prayer brings you closer to God. Working with the under privileged and the homeless is another form of prayer. Manifesting love and mercy in these areas is a tremendous example of the love and mercy of God to all.

Jesus said whatsoever you do for the least of my children you do for me. There is no greater way to experience the love and mercy of JESUS in your life than helping your neighbor. There is no greater love than this that a man gives up his life for another.

Once you reach out in love, you will notice a change in your attitude about life and spirituality. I have become more open to accepting others in spite of their theology, religion and race and culture. Consequently I feel more at ease in their presence and better about myself.

Another characteristic of love is forgiveness. There is a deep necessity to forgive yourselves and then not feel guilty. This is forgiveness. You need to be forgiven for your attitudes about others and your judgments of others can be done by asking God to forgive you. BUT in order to experience forgiveness and mercy then you have to forgive, accept and pray for all with no exception. Sometimes there needs to be a personal contact. Then the forgiveness becomes real in your experience of life. For example, personal contact is the only way peace can enter in a relationship, family, community. If you are unwilling to forgive another, you have established a block between you and the Mercy of God. The same is true of prejudice, bad judgments, fear of the poor, sick, blind, special children and the deaf.

For many people religion is something outside of them. God is up there some place. Prayer is added on when the occasion arises and the atmosphere is right. For instance, people do not pray in restaurants. Many do not sing in church but they yell at ball games. You have to keep up a certain front. Otherwise, others may judge you.

Life is what you make it. God is alive in you, in the world, in circumstances. When you enjoy life you enjoy the life of God. You may enjoy Him a little bit, by cutting corners and poor attitudes. Then again, you can enjoy life with your whole heart and soul and you then experience God with your whole heart and soul to the fullest. This is like having your cake and eating it. The freer you are in sharing with your neighbor in a Christian way, the freer you feel in God and love and prayer.

✠ **For your reflection:** *How outgoing is the practice of your faith? Do you volunteer?*

13. Understanding Your Love, Blessings of God

God made you in His image and likeness. He made you "to love." God is love and His nature is "to love." The primary purpose of your creation is "to love."

Since you are loved by God, you can now love another. "Love one another as I have loved you," Jesus said. When you reach out to another in love, one of the side effects is, you will be loved in return.

When a child is born, you love the child. The child instinctively loves you. That is the way you are created. It is your nature "to love." People may not always act that way but that does not deny the fact.

Love is of such a nature that it always desires to please more and more. A remarkable characteristic of love and often comes in surprises. Remember. the warning "you know neither the time nor is the desire "to surprise." Jesus loves surprises the hour." In fact, when you love there is no desire to hurt the other and hesitate to take advantage of their love. The more you love another, the better you feel about yourself.

I remember my Mother of God telling us, "please do not spend a lot of money on me for my birthday and Christmas. I have everything I need." Love never allows the other person to be embarrassed, or indebted. You can probably relate to many incidents in your own life. In spite of what Mom said, we bought anything we thought would please her. Love is of that nature. That is also the very nature He cannot, not love you.

If you love each other in that manner, God loves you with the same love, for He has more blessings for you than you can imagine. You often hesitate to ask for His blessings. Many people are satisfied with their spirituality and do not take advantage of God's blessings. You put a limit on gifts from the Lord. It is like getting married and saying I will love you but you cannot touch me or ask me for anything. A terrible contract for life! God desires you to ask. There are no limits on God's gifts to you.

A person who places a limit on love is like a selfish child rather than the son or daughter of a King. God has given you a gift of life. His Son Jesus came and paid for your ticket to make the journey here on earth. All God asks of you is to enjoy the trip and to love one another and His creation. He has blessed you with every spiritual gift. In the book of Proverbs it says, "The Lord's special blessing is our greatest wealth. Your work adds nothing to it." In spite of all those free blessings, the great mystery is, He constantly desires you "to ask for more."

The question is, have you tasted of the goodness of the Lord? Are you satisfied or do you desire more? The strange part is, that life is a free gift. It is a freebie. I have seen people enter a buffet restaurant. They refill their plates several times. Many things are ordered which they ordinarily would not eat if it were a la carte. Yet when it comes to the smorgasbord of free blessings of the Lord, you freeze. Why? Afraid? Ignorance? Satisfied? Lack of trust? What is needed here is trust.

During the Irish famine, a very poor relative was given a ticket to come to USA. He gathered a few shillings and bought some bread to survive on the trip. For every meal, he went to his cabin and ate the stale bread alone, as he did not have enough to share it with others. On the last day of the cruise he stood outside the dining room and watched the others eat and he desired to do so but did not have enough money. Another passenger saw him and asked him to dine with him. He said, "I do not have any money, I cannot go in to eat." The stranger said, "when you bought the ticket, that included all the three meals each day. Everything is free. It was included in the price of the ticket."

You are like that with the Lord. You have the ticket of life. Jesus paid for the journey. But you try to pay your way with your own work and endeavors. Your work adds nothing to the blessings of the Lord. Consequently, the sweet tastes of life and the joy, the happiness and compassion, are never experienced. There are loneliness and heartbreaks, anxieties and fears and so on as you ignore the invitation of the Lord to enjoy the wedding feast. The Lord told the parable about the King, who invited everyone to the wedding feast and that everything was ready. Not too many arrived. You have received the invitation. Why not enjoy it to the fullest? What is your excuse? A false notion of God prevents you from experiencing the joy and freedom of the Lord. From the precious heart of Jesus came His sincerest desire, "I have come to set you free and my joy may be in you."

Life is like it is because you make it so. It is not the fault of God. Your attitudes as you rise in the morning set the tone of the day. I can rise in the morning with a prayer that it will be a great day or I can get up and go through the motions. I had an aisle seat in a commuter plane from Washington. It was a glorious ride and the sun and clouds were beautiful. The passenger near the window drew the shade. We rode in darkness. It reminded me of life in the spiritual world. The gifts of life and the invitations of God are all around and they are passed over. I remember my Mother saying to me when I returned from a wedding or golf or a trip, "John, did you have a good time? Did you enjoy yourself?" I imagine God will ask the same question. In fact, He may even say, "why did you waste so much time since my Son paid your way is similar to someone giving you orchestra seats at Shea's Buffalo, and you do not use them.

Your life is in your hands, how are you going to live each day? Jesus paid the price. He did not count the cost. You are worth it to Him.

✠ **For your reflection:** *Do you see life as a free gift and blessing from God?*

14. **Adventure in Faith**

It is necessary to understand life in order to enjoy it to the fullest. When you are brought up in a certain way, education, culture, that is all you know. It is your condition. Life dictates that there are other cultures, countries, traditions which are as good as, or better than, the way you have been conditioned, trained and educated. There is more to God and life and spirituality and prayer than meets your eyes. God is infinite. Jesus is the Way for every person, including you. I have included one of my many adventures with the hope that it will inspire you to begin your journey. Here is one of my many adventures. You also have a journey.

Many years ago, I met Lillian Bernas. Lillian has the gift of the stigmata, similar to Padre Pio and St. Francis. Every first Friday for one year, she suffered and bled as Jesus did on the cross. I witnessed it many months in her home in Canada. She manifests the sufferings of Jesus on Good Fridays.

I asked permission of our Bishop Henry Mansell and he allowed me to invite her to speak at St. Michael's. I then invited her to give a talk at St. Michael's on Sunday, November 11. We started with a rosary at 4:30 followed by Mass and a talk. She is known as a "victim soul" for Christ. She always suffers the pain to make up for the sins of many. She has been examined by the Canadian Bishops and found to be "Believable." This means that the manifestations are not of natural origin in any way. We are privileged to have her with us. The gift of the stigmata is rarely given. You may never have another chance to listen to her. Here is an opportunity to grow. Lilian lives next door in Canada. People traveled miles to witness Padre Pio in Italy. She is within an hour of Buffalo.

You only have to cross the border. It gave me a startling experience of the cross, observing Lillian bleeding and praying. Everyone is not so called. It is a very special gift of God rarely granted in the history of the saints. Lillian will pray with anyone who so desires after her presentations. She will be giving lectures in many churches on the mercy of the Lord. If you have the opportunity, attend one or more of her lectures.

When you were created in the image and likeness of God, you were made in a certain way and given a name and destiny by God. You have an obligation in life to discern your capabilities and use them to share in the work of salvation. Everyone, no matter who they are, has a purpose in fulfilling the scheme and pattern of life. You cannot leave it to someone else. Only you, with your personality, can fulfill the role. The difficulty is, you do not believe in your own importance or the value of your efforts. There are no answers to life. Only God knows the answers. You need to trust and to understand that God alone gives the increase.

Lillian had to change her way of life and give herself to God completely. She was finally asked to quit her job and live in the trust of the Lord. All you are asked to do, is find yourself and do what you are able, in the circumstances in which you live. To be happy and fulfilled in Christ goes beyond yourself, as the scriptures proclaim. Enough is not good enough.

You treat your spiritual life similar to your natural way of acting. If you always do the same things, go on the same vacation every year, eat the same menu when you dine out, you are in a rut. So when it comes to the spiritual life, you never change, try anything new, never experience other forms of prayer. You will never experience the great things the Lord has in store for you. You are traveling second class when you have a first class ticket in this beautiful journey called life. You are the loser.

I never wanted to be a loser. I tried out, in high school, for the school play. I thought it would be neat to be on the stage. So I tried. I failed miserably. I did not quit living. I tried other things and excelled. I learned something from the failure.

The same is true in the spiritual life. If you try something and it does not work, you just move on. That is growth. I receive spiritual books to read and I start them. Some I finish and some I put aside for future reading.

Never prejudge anything. If you listen to the experiences of others, do not allow them to make the decisions of life for you. It is your life. It is your decision. Make up your own mind. To make your own decision, it is necessary to try it yourself. Try it now and see what happens. The Lord has a purpose in life for you. You are an essential cog in His framework of life. No one can take your place for you are unique. Only you can fill in the space in the tapestry of life. Your spiritual life is necessary to complete your journey. It is a hunger which needs to be satisfied to be happy.

My Mother was a great example for loving life in her own way. Before St. Joseph's Hospital broke ground, my Mother and many other women sold pencils from door to door. Money made on the pencils went to Fr. Justin for plans and so on. Mother moved out in faith and believed in the cause. Look at the hospital today. Mom took much teasing for selling pencils but she stuck to her guns. She had great faith in the Little Flower. She believed in the prayer and said it all the time. She spread the devotion. Many remarkable graces and roses were given to her in response to her prayer. On a number of occasions, when I entered the house, it was filled with the scent of roses, especially her bedroom. I asked Mom did someone send you roses? She would say no one sent roses except the Little Flower. Mom had her own spirituality. Our home had beautiful holy pictures in every room. She even made going to church fun. We would walk to church in the morning. We walked, then she would suddenly start to run. Then she would stop when we got near. Mother made life interesting, even when we went for a family ride in the car.

Your life is in your hands. You are the only one responsible for your relationship to the Lord. You can enjoy life or make life a drudgery. For me, I do not want to sit on the bench. I desire to be an active player.

✠ For your reflection:

How do you react to new opportunities to grow spiritually? Have you ever tried to experience more of the love of God? Retreats? Bible classes? Days of recollection? Missions? Holy Hours? Good Reading?

Fr. John & brother Herb - 1930

15. **The Gift of Life – Blessings**

You were given the gift of life to discover who you are and to determine the role you need to play in the Kingdom of God. Discover these and then go into action. Make life happen. That is where God is. I came to my senses in college and accepted the challenge of the Lord to leave school and my job at DuPont to study for the priesthood. I had to leave my part time job at DuPont to take summer school.

The Lord is very generous in His blessings to His children. Life is given, to let you share in His blessings. Too often, they are misused and over looked. Every morning I pray, "Almighty God, bless me indeed." I ask Him to bless me. Can you believe that the Lord is delighted to bless you? In confession you say, "Bless me Father." Do you know what that means? You are in sin, you are on the outs, yet you ask the Lord to bless you.

Many years ago, some friends went to the Holy Land and returned with a very beautiful gift. It was a hand carved dove hung on a string of carved small beads to wear. It was admired by everyone. One day the woman who gave it to me asked, "Fr. John, do you like the gift I gave you from the Holy Land?" I said, "Yes I do." Then she said, "Why don't you wear it?" To say the least I was really embarrassed. It is similar to receiving a birthday present or a Christmas gift and it is never used. She taught me a great lesson of life. In order to appreciate life, it is necessary to accept life and enjoy it and be ready for change. I remember when I was young, I bought a marvelous pair of racing skates. In those days we named them long tubes. I loved those skates and enjoyed hours of speed skating. One winter, I was ready to go ice-skating and tried on the skates. To my surprise they were too small. I had to give them to my brother. I did not want to give in to the size of the skates and still tried them on but they hurt. I had to buy another pair. Life is like that. The spiritual life is the same. For growth, change has to take place. Anything that does not die or change is plastic. God is alive. God is love. Love is not static. Love is dynamic. He is the God of the living. Everything changes. Yesterday is different from today. Yesterday cannot be brought back to life. Today is the day the Lord has made.

I remember the first year in the Society of Jesus. On Christmas Eve, all the new men were asleep in the dormitory. It was a lonesome feeling, being away from home, as I went to bed. At midnight, to my total surprise, I was awakened by a male chorus of the older men singing Christmas hymns. It sounded like angels from heaven. Time as it was stood still. In all of the later years in the Society, there was nothing ever like those same feelings. The total surprise and unawareness, I can still recall, but cannot recapture the feelings that evening. Life changes, nothing is the same. There was no use trying to repeat it, for I changed, the circumstances changed. I thank God for the memory.

If you are grounded in security and afraid to grow, and just plain satisfied, life will just pass you by. Your spiritual life is the same. If you are afraid to grow in your interior life and do not feed it, the many blessings of the Lord will not fall upon you. It would be like walking in the rain with a huge umbrella.

To be happy and to enjoy life, you have to create it physically and spiritually. To wait for anything else or someone else to make you happy is vanity and a false assumption and passivity. No one owes it to you, the world does not owe it to you, and life does not owe you a living. Don't waste your life by waiting for love and happiness. Life and love take personal work. You have the power of creation. You have to make it happen.

No one can do your praying for you. No one can give you an experience in prayer. Reading books and not putting ideas into action is almost a waste of time. All the reading is in vain, if you are not open to some change and action. Knowledge alone does not make a good Christian. Because the seal blows a trumpet, does not make it a musician. The Lord awaits your response to His gift of life. What are your gifts? Life is a blessing and your life is a free gift. ASK God for His blessings and USE them and ENJOY them. God gives you a season pass to all His blessings. Opportunity knocks only once. To make God laugh, plan to put things off until later. Later may never come for you. You cannot plan God. Take advantage of every day. Enjoy the blessings of God. It is necessary to enjoy every moment. Never take tomorrow for granted. Do not wait for the time to be just right to do something. It seldom or ever happens. You have to make the right time. Life does not wait for you.

In the story of the wedding feast, the King sent personal invitations. The King announced, that the feast was ready, the foods prepared, come and celebrate with me. All had excuses. The blessings of the Lord are signed and sealed and packaged for you. You need to be present to receive them. Now is the time. Do not allow life to pass you by. The reality is that life is over before you realize it. Time gets shorter every minute

✟ **For your reflection:** *What is your response? He patiently awaits your personal reply. RSVP. Do you have sufficient faith and trust in God to grow?*

16. **Illusion**

The definition of an illusion: a misconception, false impression, a misconception, which fails to give the true character of the thing or idea perceived. This is true of life. You are deceived in advertisements, pretty names for false things [prochoice], fear of God and what He will send you, in marriage I'll change the other and so on.

How do you treat the gift of the Lord? Jesus invites you to the wedding feast, the gift of life. Do you recognize the value of the personal invitation? It is free. Are you proud of it? Do you use it as God has intended? How do you use the gift of time? Faith?

I remember when I was on a cruise, the woman in charge of entertainment used to say every evening "enjoy yourself, it is your vacation, you paid for it." God says "enjoy yourself, it is your life, My Son paid for it." What is your excuse? Modern society has filled you and maneuvered you to living an insecure life. You have been led to believe that you can get along without God and that you can do anything you so desire. You are indifferent to God. The Kingdom is no longer your priority. Success, honor, power, riches have become your way of life. Society has drilled you to live a dissatisfied life. It teaches you that fulfillment depends on some sort of condition. Every ad insists they have a better product. If you want to be happy, then buy these jeans. If you desire to be alluring, then get this perfume. If you desire to be kissable, then use this lip stick. Consequently, the way you developed your thinking and feelings you educated yourselves to believe, that happiness exists somewhere outside of you and totally dependent upon the condition "IF." That is an illusion. You become like sleep walkers. The sad part is you do not recognize your condition and do not know the sweet taste of life. Business grows rich on your dissatisfaction. You believe that this is the only way to live to be completely happy. It is sad. Consequently, you do not recognize the value of the invitation sent by the King who has your interest at heart and not business and profit. Time has no value in your eyes.

You have faith and say you trust in God but are filled with suspicions. There is a fear that God will send you things you do not like. You believe He is too busy to listen to your prayers that it is not right to ask God for little things. To be open to the blessings of the Lord, it is necessary to trust in God that He is a faithful Father. Jesus said, "Ask anything in my name and the Father will give it to you." It is necessary to trust and know that God will answer your prayers. It is necessary to enter into prayer with confidence. Otherwise, do not pray. If you pray, do not worry and if you worry, do not pray. I pray for parking spots and thank God for finding them. Very successful.

God is more willing to give things than you are to receive them. In fact, He has to hold back, lest you be deceived. Frequently parents are the same. They desire to give their children everything they ask. However, for the good of the children the gift is not given. Why do you believe that God is less than willing to open the abundance of the Kingdom for you? He told you, "Seek first the Kingdom of God and all things will be given to you." Don't you trust in the Word of the Lord? What type of life is that, in which you do not trust?

His generosity and desire to share are spoken in the Scriptures. In Deuteronomy 28,3 "You will be blessed in the city and blessed in the country. You will be blessed when you go in and you will be blessed when you go out." What more do you desire God to tell you?

It is necessary to get rid of any doubts that limit His generosity and His goodness. He is an infinite God and He does not keep any ledger about what He has given you. Every day is a new day. Like any loving Father, He cares for your heart and interests. My Dad frequently took me aside and desired to hear what my expectations were in life. God is the same. Ask for what you need and wait and see what happens. He has a personal interest in your way of life. When you have a more positive attitude about yourself, you will begin to see God with a more positive attitude. It will aid you in mitigating the wrong concepts of God. Slowly the idea of a God, Who loves you unconditionally, will wake you up to this wonderful gift of life. You will wonder why you did not perceive this earlier.

You will see that God dwells within you. It is not necessary to look outside of yourself to find God. God and love and happiness exist within you. If you cannot discover them within yourself, you will never find them anywhere. God has not left you an orphan. He did not place you here at this time without preparing you for the difficulties you face. He has given you every spiritual gift. They all exist within you. It is up to your initiative and love of life to discover them and enjoy this beautiful existence of human life. If you find difficulty ask God to come to your aid. Do not be fooled by the culture of the modern world. It is mostly out to deceive.

✛ **For your reflection:** *Why do you hesitate to ask Jesus for little things? ASK for what you desire.*

17. **God Created You a Lover**

God made you a lover. How do I know? God made you in His own image and likeness, and God is love. Therefore, you are a lover and God dwells within you. Look at yourself and you will see how you felt a great satisfaction in helping another. When you helped someone, you felt very good. God sees Himself in you, when you act as He did, in loving and reaching out to others. Your life and prayer life, open your heart to appreciate the gifts that God has given you. When you discover them, you will begin to realize and experience God dwelling within you. Your whole attitude about life, about God, about others, will give you a very peaceful, relaxing attitude. Things and people will disturb you less. Your blood pressure will even lower. You may even feel healthier and less nervous. You will go from a nervous attitude about life to a more confident person. All this happened to me as time went on.

I said "to myself" that if I am made in the image and likeness of God and He dwells in me, then I must have some good qualities. But, since I am human, I must have some negative qualities. So I sat down and tried to write some of my good qualities on a sheet of paper. Then I wrote my negative qualities on a sheet of paper. I found out that it was easier to find negative qualities then positive. I had a lot of work to do. So, I prayed and tried to see me as God sees me. Slowly I dropped my quick judgment of others, my 'get even temper' behind the wheel, my wasting of time, and my prejudices. I was amazed how much better I felt about myself as many of these negative things were dropped. I changed my entire attitude about God. I began to see Him as a loving God and a merciful God. To love, takes hard work as you know.

I mentioned to you at the beginning that Thomas Merton wrote, "In order to grow in love of God and holiness, it is necessary to drop all the old notions and attitudes and begin again." I hope you begin to see this.

Once you discover God within you and that you are a lover, you will discover God in others, circumstances, creation and hopefully in the people with whom you have difficulty. You will be more accepting of others, there will be less prejudice, and even less fear. You will learn little by little that "All is Well." You may even experience how much you are in the Hands of God. You now know the secret of the saints. Consult Julian of Norwich, the 13the century mystic. She really was the first modern woman. Read her book "Showings of Julian of Norwich." Fantastic reading. Down to earth spirituality.

I prayed and was intrigued by the statement that we are created in the image and likeness of God. If that is true, then God is going to take care of me. I have His stamp of approval. I enjoy working in wood. When a piece is finished, I am proud of it. Then I try to give it to someone who will appreciate the effort. If I am so careful with what I create, how much more does God care for me?

He made me and formed me and called me by name. When He saw me, He said that John is good. Consequently, I began to look at my physical self with my good qualities and faults. Jesus said I was good and I began to tell myself the same thing even though I did not feel it. I did not want to tell Jesus that He made a mistake.

I had to work on my own self image. If God saw me as good, why did I not see the same? Every morning I looked into the mirror and said that God loves me and Jesus loves me. Many times, I have heard people say I wish I had a deeper faith. One of the most perfect acts of faith is to say, "I am beautiful in the eyes of Christ" and to believe in yourself. Try it and see what it does for you and be aware of your feelings. Your mistaken notions of God will disappear and you will slowly realize that He really loves you as you are. To increase in faith, you need to believe in yourself.

⊕ **For your reflection:** *How do you honestly see your self-image? Describe it? Do you realize that Jesus loves you?*

Marriage Encouter group

18. Happiness

Another tremendous illusion in your lives is, happiness exists somewhere outside of you. I was the same. I desired a pair of new skates and I'd be the happiest kid on the block. It was a thrill when I received them but it did not last long. Soon I wanted something else. I desired my parents to allow me to play football. I played and was thrilled but the feeling did not last and soon my heart was set on something else. You desire to get married and believe that if you meet the right person, happiness will be yours forever. What happened? You desire your children to go to Church and this will make you happy. They don't respond. Something else soon pops up. You say that you will be happy, if you could get a new job. It is a thrill when those things are achieved but it does not last. Soon your heart meets reality and it wants something else or better. You discover by experience, that happiness in your life never lasts, for it always depends on something else to happen. Check out your own life style. Are you really happy? Do you see it is true, that happiness does not exist outside of you?

As long as there are loneliness, despair, guilt, prejudice, hatred, doubts, distrust, greed, selfishness, anger, boredom and the like, there is no happiness. The scripture says that perfect love casts out all fear. Happiness exists in you. Happiness does not depend upon any outside influence. You cannot search for happiness. You already have it. If you say that you cannot be happy unless you possess something or some person, you will never be happy. You will never find happiness because it already exists in you.

Desire and expectations are the roots of unhappiness. This does not mean that you do not have desires and expectations. You cannot go through life without them. That would be inhuman. But if you say that you will not be happy unless your expectations and desire are met, that is wrong. The Lord did not create you dependent upon anyone or any thing to achieve happiness. The Lord did not make you an orphan. You have all the gifts necessary within you to live happily and in peace. It is necessary to understand those desires and see that you can be at peace. If someone loves you, fine. If someone does not love you, fine. If you want to be loved, then love someone yourself. If you have something, fine, if you do not have something, fine. It is necessary to be indifferent to all. The secret is to be content. You do not reject anything and you do not hanker for anything. St. Paul says, "I know how to have a good meal and I know how to be hungry."

This is living a life of faith. It is following God's will. Just take things as they are and to imitate the birds in the sky and lilies in the field, to take what comes and to let go of what is transient. This is faith. The Lord gives and the

Lord takes away. It is necessary to keep your priorities straight. If you can do that you will be at peace, content and happy.

I am going to repeat a story I heard. Give this deep thought. When the archer shoots at a target, he has all his skills. When he shoots for the brass ring, he is already nervous. When he shoots for gold, he goes out of his mind. His skills are the same but his heart is on the prize. He is divided. He values the prize more than the target. In sports it is called choking. Desire for life, can ruin life.

Life is like a river, it comes and goes, it flows. You cannot cling to life, to the past nor to the present. When you attend a symphony, it has a beginning and an end. It is necessary to listen to every note and every chord to enjoy its beauty. If you cling to a note or chord, you miss the beauty of the symphony.

Life is like that. If your expectations and desires are so overwhelming that it takes all your strength, you are not really living. You are missing your goal in life. Consequently your priorities must always be in order. A moment wasted is a moment of joy lost. When your health, work and prayer are in harmony you will discover happiness. Joy will be yours. You know from experience that when work is very consuming, your relationship suffers and so does your prayer and health. If you spend too much time in prayer, your work cannot be accomplished. If you neglect your own body and misuse it, the other things will suffer. I know it is true of me. I can get so busy in the morning that I put off my prayers. It results in performing them late at night or not at all. I learn from experience, what I can do and what I can't do. I need prayer to discern the needs of each day, to be at peace every day and night. Happiness comes when you least expect it. It cannot be bought or bargained. It is a gift from God because of whom and what you are. Live in the present moment and you will experience the peace, love and joy of God. You will be happy.

When you discover that you are not at peace, look for the trouble in your priorities. When they get upset and the Kingdom of God is not first, you have lost the Lord. Your concerns and worries take over and ruin your peace and happiness.

✠ **For your reflection:** *List in detail the blessings in your life? In which way does this change your attitudes?*

19. Image and Likeness of God

The statement that we are made in the image and likeness of God, always mystifies and thrills me. I am created in the image and likeness of God. You are made in the image and likeness of God. We are different. Your neighbor is made in the image and likeness of God. The Korean is made in the image and likeness of God. The Africans are made in the image and likeness of God. The Muslim is made in the image and likeness of God. The saint and the sinner are made in the image and likeness of God. All over creation for centuries, all are made in the image and likeness of God. We are all made for the same purpose, namely "to love." Happiness exists in every person and few can find it. TO MY UTTER AMAZEMENT, EVERYONE IS DIFFERENT, YET WE WERE ALL MADE "TO LOVE."

What kind of God is this that is so powerful and so imaginative, that He can create millions of people all very differently? Yet we all are created for the same purpose "to love." You were created in love and by love "to love." That is God's plan for you.

Another amazing feature of God is this, He loves every bit of His creation and called everything good. Even though many do not love Him and many do not see good in the world, God still loves everyone and everything.

In His tremendous love He added an awesome gift of amazing power and strength, a free will. You can do anything you desire with His gifts. He gave very few instructions as to how to use these gifts. All He said is "love one another." Everything He desired of you is contained in the commandment to love each other and not to hurt each other. In doing so you will be achieving the gifts to enjoy life. He is like any other good parent. He wants everyone to have the best and not get hurt or hurt anyone else. Translated, that means in plain language, to respect your body and soul and to respect your neighbor. SIMPLE INSTRUCTIONS. What a sacrifice of our Creator to give away His own handiwork. He loves and allows you to use it or misuse it. That is true love.

Let me tell you a parable, a real story. One of the most imaginative phrases in the English language is "Once upon a time." Did you ever think of it?

Once upon a time, I visited a friend's house. He was cleaning out the garage. In the junk pile was a red flyer wagon. It brought back fond memories when my parents bought me one for Christmas. On the old junky wagon were four good wheels with white tires. Good wheels are hard to find. The wagon was in terrible shape, very rusty and broken. I saw some good in it. God is like that with you. He always sees good in you, no matter what you think or believe or what you have done.

When I saw it, I liked the wheels. So, I asked if I could take the wagon. When I arrived home, I could picture the wagon completely fixed. I planned to fix it up and give it to the day care center in our parish. Fortunately I did not tell them. All winter long I sanded and ground away with el-

The red wagon

ectric grinding wheels. I had one of the retired men around the church help me and we worked. It was sanded to the bare steel. We were proud of our results. Then I gave it two coats of rust proof paint and sanded after each layer. Then I gave it four coats of a brilliant red enamel. It was sanded after each coat of paint. I then topped it off with two coats of polyurethane vanish. It looked like new. Then I had a decal company make me "RADIO FLYER------90", in white. I pasted one on both sides of the wagon. It was completed with another coat of varnish. It looked like a million dollars.

NOW LISTEN to this. When I began the project, I intended to give it away but in the process of working on the wagon, I fell in love with the wagon and could not give it away. It is now in my bedroom filled with beanie babies. I call them my prayer group. The picture is in the book.

I loved my work so much that I could not give it away. But God created you with much less work and gave you away to enjoy life and the gifts that He gives to you. That is true unconditional love. If you cannot perceive that Jesus loves you and if you refuse to give up mistaken notions of Him, you will never achieve happiness and peace. You will always live with fear, anxiety, worry, loneliness and so on. It is only when you realize that Jesus has a personal interest in you, then and then only, will you be free and happiness will be yours. As Jesus said, "you cannot put new wine into old wineskins." To experience your gifts, it is necessary to get rid of the extra baggage. Rid yourselves of worry and anxieties.

In life when you are at peace and are happy, it is a pretty certain sign that the Lord is with you and that you are doing His work. It leaves you with a certain amount of satisfaction. This positive attitude then affects all those around you. You are a sign of God's goodness and love. You are created to love, to love another and God's creation.

✠ **For your reflection:** *What does the description that "you are made in the image and likeness of God," mean to you?*

20. **Children of God**

You know that God loves you. He created you in His own image and likeness and God is love. Then, you often wonder how much does He love you. Well for that reason you can look into the scriptures. In the book of Romans you can find some testimony, 8: 14, "For those who are led by the Spirit of God, are children of God. For you did not receive a spirit of slavery to fall back into fear, but you received a spirit of adoption, through which you cry, "Abba, Father!" "The Spirit itself bears witnesses with your spirit that you are children of God, and if children, then heirs, heirs of God and joint heirs with Christ, if you suffer with him so that you may also be glorified with him."

You know that sometimes you say you do not believe, unless you understand. It is just the opposite. You need to believe, in order to understand. You need to believe that God is your Father and as St. Paul writes, you may call Him "ABBA" that is Father. In a real sense, He is "Daddy" but that term is sort of childish. As an adult you use a more mature name. You are a child of God. God is your Father.

Since you are a child of God, God loves you as He loves His Son Jesus. He pours forth His graces on you with the same intensity and concern. He never abandons you no matter what the circumstances. He constantly loves you and always wishes you the best. He desires that you always go first class and not consider yourself unworthy. You are an adopted child. Jesus is a natural child of the same Father as you. Adopted children have the same rights in a family as a natural child.

Once upon a time there was a young girl in a playground. Some children were constantly teasing her about being adopted. She took it for a little time and then she said: "When you were born, your parents had to accept you. They had no choice. You were their gift. My parents saw me, loved me and chose me." The Father loves Jesus and Jesus loves the Father. The Father loves you and you should love the Father. My parents saw me, loved me. I love my parents.

One of the amazing characteristics of God is, God chose you. You did not choose Him. He loved you first, before you loved Him. He now desires that you grow in love of Him and the rest of His children.

St. Paul says "you did not receive a spirit of slavery to fall back into fear but you received a spirit of adoption, through which you cry, "Abba," Father. Since you are a child of God, you are an heir of God and coheir with Christ. If you suffer with Him and love Him, then you may also be glorified with Him."

All the graces, blessings, rewards, support, honor, dignity, titles, angels and all that which belongs to the Father are yours. You are an heir of a Kingdom.

It is the Father's Kingdom. It now belongs to you. You have the title of prince or a princess. If the God you create in your own mind does not make you a prince or princess, then you adore the wrong God. The Kingdom is your rightful claim. A dwelling place is being made for you with your desires in mind. Just as God the Father loves Jesus, so He loves you. All He asks of you is love and respect yourself and love and respect your neighbor in the same way. Jesus is your model.

If your notion and ideas of God do not leave you with the feeling that you are a prince or princess, you are in the right church but the wrong pew. You are a child of God. He has adopted you. He loves you. You need to believe in yourself. This act of believing in yourself that you are beautiful in God's sight and a child of God, is a great act of faith. You need to believe in yourself in order to understand yourself. No matter what you think of yourself, God sees you as beautiful. God does not judge you as you judge yourself. The Lord is merciful. Think positive and rid yourself of the negative. You are a prize possession. Your Father is the Greatest. However, The Father loves Jesus and Jesus loves the Father. The Father loves you and you should love the Father. You live in His Kingdom of love.

⊕ **For your reflection:** *What does it mean to you to be an adopted child of God?*

21. **Child of God**

By this time you should have the belief that God loves you. All the other notions and feelings place conditions on you. God does not place conditions on His love. God loves you unconditionally and unless you completely come to believe this, you will never understand the beautiful gifts of mercy and forgiveness which are given to you.

You are loved by God. God loves you just as He loves His Son Jesus, because God is love. Love exists within you. Therefore, experience as much love as possible. The more you take in the more you can love another. You have to be able to say from the heart "God loves me." Paul declared this, "He loved me." John defined himself as the "Disciple whom Jesus loved." A Christian is a person who can truly say, "Jesus loves me." For instance if I do not experience the love of my brother whom I see, how can I experience the love of God whom I do not see? You are all children of God. You are all princes or princesses in a Kingdom in which God is your Father. If I ask a child "Do you know that Jesus loves you," the child immediately answers or nods his/her head "yes." If I ask an adult, "do you know that Jesus loves you?" he takes his time in responding and then say "I hope so." Why the different answers?

You are children in the sight of God. You live and act in the same manner as you believe. Your ideas of God also determine the way you act. You are filled with the doctrines of the world which have drowned out the love of God. Children are free. They possess the gift, which Jesus desires to share with you "FREEDOM." For instance the children feel loved, they are secure, they instinctively rely on their Mommy and Daddy. Jesus came to SET YOU FREE. However you thought that you could do better by yourselves and just see what happened to you and the world. You lost your trust and balance. Why did you change from being a little child?

Achievement and success in life do not give you security in life. The off shoot is anxiety and worry. You worry that you may lose it. Success breeds success and the more success you achieve the more anxiety enters. You are never free. Success has to be balanced in life. You suffer because others love you for your achievement rather than your person. Success tells you that your work is fine, while love tells you that you are fine. This is the ultimate satisfaction of your person. You want to be loved for your own sake. You desire to be loved as you are, a child of God. You are created "to love." If you first love another, then the rest will follow. You are loved if you love first. Nothing can buy love and happiness.

God's depth of love is unconditional. It does not depend on your success or achievements. You are loved for yourself. This gives you security, the satisfaction, the safety of being loved for your own sake. Therefore, you are not dependent on any success or failure for your well being. You are independent and free. Consequently, the conclusion is to LOVE OTHERS and experience their love in return. Take in all the love you can and this will give you security, peace, balance and freedom. Let God love you. Let your work and success bless you. Give all the glory to God. Do not allow money, greed, power, successes become your gods of life. Those elements do not bring you love and happiness, only sorrow and grief. Life is too short and precious to waste on earthly and passing things. Only love is important.

You are important and Jesus knew that life can be difficult. Therefore, He came to show you the way. You really do not have to achieve anything. All Jesus desires, is your effort to be good and try to love your neighbor. It is in that effort that Jesus begins to open hearts to love. Your effort is similar to a child who draws a picture for his Mom. You may have to guess at the picture but you praise the child for his effort and love. You are all the children of God. Your works and efforts accomplished in love, earn the praise of God whether you were successful or not. This includes your failures in time of temptation. He blesses the efforts.

✠ **For your reflection:** *The above thoughts are what Jesus meant when He said, "Unless you become like little children you will not enter the Kingdom of Heaven." How does that statement affect you?*

22. **Love Within Your Grasp**

You believe that "God is love." Who is this God? When Moses asked God, "Show me your glory" God responded, "The Lord, the Lord God, merciful and gracious, long suffering and abounding in goodness and truth." If you have a lower opinion of God, wake up to life and realize there is more to life than you have been experiencing. It is of the very nature of God to posses so much kindness and goodness in abundance that it overflows into your lives. It is beyond your wildest imagination to believe that God could be so good to you. WHY? Don't you understand, that the love of God is UNCONDITIONAL? Instead of placing your trust in God, you place your trust in the ideas of the world, the illusions and half-truths. Do not underestimate the love of God for you.

You may recall that I mentioned the word "balance" previously. "Balance" means that your priorities must be in order. You need to understand your person, the circumstances in which you live, your obligations to God and family and life and maintain common sense. It is your life. You alone are responsible. Do not allow your happiness to depend on the expectations of others or your achievements. Discover happiness in yourself. For instance, what is the reason that most motivates you in leading your life? Is it not "what will the neighbors think?" There are those who are afraid to profess their faith because the neighbors may think they are holy. People do not sing in church because others may think they are showing off. People dress to please their neighbor. Look at peer pressure in the teens. Look at yourself. How many times do you act and say things just to make a good impression on others? How many times would you really enjoy being different or would rather miss a function? How many occasions have you acted in a manner the neighbors expect of you? You have handed over to your neighbor power over you. When you react to someone cutting you off on the expressway, you have handed over to that person power to control you. Children are free. They just act out. If I acted, the way others expected of me, I would be extremely limited. I would not be free. Jesus came to set you free. You need to use common sense.

It is necessary to have balance in life. Use your common sense, which is a grace of God, to help you in your daily tasks. Do not be afraid to ask God even for the tiniest thing. Some things may sound ridiculous to you, but to others they make sense. Ask! God is not so far away that He would not hear you or pay attention to you.

I went shopping in a toy department. I noticed children would grab a toy and say "Mommy I want this." If they get it or not depended on Mom. They asked. Ask God for anything, and if it is in His will, your request will be answered. He is a loving God. BUT, if you do not ask, you haven't any reason to blame God for your unhappiness in your life. Ask God to help you understand. Poor God, He gets blamed for everything.

It is an act faith to forget the past and say, "Jesus loves me." This is the sign of a real Christian. Believe and declare that God is Love. God's love is unlimited. It is boundless. Your credit card is forever and you may use it for anything. Jesus pays for your credit card. Nothing is ever subtracted from it. God does not keep books. All He does is to love you. The way to give thanks to God is to love yourself and love your neighbor. This way of acting is the perfect prayer. Let nothing stand in the way of loving another. You will have to forgive your enemies and the past. Ask God to help. It requires a miracle of grace to ask for forgiveness. Receive the sacrament of penance and the Eucharist. These give you the strength to lead a good Christian life.

You are never beyond the love of God. He is always with you. However, to experience His love it is necessary to do something, such as prayer, receive the sacraments, ask for forgiveness, come to the aid of your neighbor, perform works of mercy and so on. It is in the reaching out that Jesus sees your effort and you begin to experience His love. You begin to feel secure and at peace. A certain sense of self -confidence begins to warm your spirit.

✝ **For your reflection:** *Have you ever experienced the love of Jesus? Can you describe your feelings?*

23. **God is Love**

It is necessary to have the right notion, the correct picture of God in your mind and heart. Otherwise, how would you know if it is God when you meet Him or when and if He talks to you? For instance, if you had the incorrect picture or the wrong concept of the President of the USA, how would you recognize him? The Scribes and the Pharisees had the wrong concepts of Jesus. When Jesus came they did not recognize Him and eventually crucified Him. They were expecting someone different. How often do you do the same thing? You often act on the wrong assumption.

You actually live in the love of God. His love surrounds you all the time. There is never a moment when you are out of His love. It is like being in the sun on a cloudless sky. There is no way of seeking relief from the sun. It shines on you all the time. God gives you the very same love He gives to His Son Jesus. You are His special children. All He desires is to love you and give you the best deal. If you reach out for less, do not blame the Lord. He desires you to go first class. It is necessary to be able to recognize God in your daily life and daily actions. When you have the wrong concepts, ideas, pictures, you will miss the Lord. You will never be happy. I am going to tell you a parable. You are in this story. There was a little fish swimming in the ocean. His great desire in life was to swim in the ocean. He believed if he found the ocean he would be the happiest fish alive. He swam around and around, up and down for weeks and months. He was ready to give up. Finally, he met a great big fish and he thought, that old fish must have found the ocean in his day and maybe he will tell me where it is. So he swam up to the old fish and said, "Sir, I see you are old fish, you must have seen and been in the ocean in your day. Please tell me where I can find it and I will be the happiest fish alive." The old fish said to the little fish, "Why sir, you are swimming in the ocean," "Oh no," said the little fish "I am only swimming in the water," and he sadly swam away.

The little fish had the wrong concept of "Ocean" and even when he was swimming in the ocean, he thought it was only "water." That is the way with those who have the wrong or mistaken notion of God. You miss God in your life.

The Disciples on the road to Emmaus did not recognize Jesus for the entire journey. Their eyes were opened only when they changed their viewpoint. Then they recognized Jesus. The same is true for all who have the mistaken notions of Jesus. You are engulfed in the love of God. You eat, drink and sleep in His love, every moment of every day. In spite of that, you have not opened your eyes to see.

If you look for God outside of yourself, in church, in circumstances of life, in prayer, in others, you will never find Him unless you recognize God in yourself first. It is necessary to know who He is, in your notions, in your attitudes, in your thoughts. If you know God as love and that He loves you, you are on your way to waking up to life and God.

All you have to do is open your eyes and there is God. He is not in yesterday and not in tomorrow. He is in today and in you, even now as you read.

The King constantly invites you to the palatial wedding feast. He says, "On this mountain the Lord of hosts will provide for all peoples, a feast of rich food and choice wines, juicy rich food and pure choice wines. This is the Lord for whom we looked, let us rejoice and be glad that He has saved us." Isa. 25-6

God is love. God is good. God is generous. God is compassionate. God is merciful. God is in the present moment, this instant, this incident, this conversation and this task. He is not in yesterday and He is not in tomorrow. You have to recognize God now, this very moment, in this reading. He loves you wherever you are, no matter what you are doing, thinking or believing. Pray for the gift to see Jesus as you go through your day.

✠ **For your reflection:** *Do you recognize God in the course of the day? How do you know that it is God?*

Fr. John and Sr. Noreen in Ireland

24. **Christmas Love**

To begin with, Jesus loves you, He always forgives you, you get new life. On Christmas is Jesus born, comes into the world to bring you peace and love. Love is a sharing of love which brings new life. That is the story of Christmas.

Many years ago I married a couple. They anxiously awaited a child and did everything possible to achieve their dream. Nothing happened. After waiting 17 long years, they were notified that if they came to Albany in two days, they will be given a new baby two days old. They did as they were told. On the fourth day, I went to visit the couple. I walked in the back door and the mother was sitting in the family room holding the baby and just looking in awe and wonder at the sight. She never looked up at me, never said a word for about three or four minutes. Finally, she turned and said, "Father would you like to hold the baby." I was afraid, for I never had that experience in life, so I sat down on the couch. She brought the baby over and laid her in my arms. I just looked at the baby in awe and wonder. I whispered, "Jesus loves you, play with the angels."

Mary, the Mother of Jesus, was visited by an angel and told not to fear that she would soon have a child and he will be called "Jesus" and the Lord God will give him the Kingdom of David. I wonder what went through her mind and heart? How and where would He be born? Who would be there? What kind of a reception will He have? Is our home ready for such an event? You know what took place. He was born in poverty. There was no place to stay. He was born in a stable and laid in a manger used for animal feed. He was clothed in swaddling clothes. I imagine His Mother held Him in her arms and just looked at this child in wonder and awe. What could have gone through her heart as she felt this gift?

By this act she became the Mother of God and the Mother of all of us. We are all brothers and sisters of Jesus and adopted children of God. We have all the rights of the Kingdom as Jesus.

Jesus in His love gave Himself to you that you could have new life. This is the description of love. Love is the sharing of self with another that the other may gain new life. You are all called to do that.

When you go to Holy Communion, you hold in your hand the real Jesus. You hold Him in your arms and heart. You can look at Him with wonder and awe. That is prayer. That is love. When you pray before the exposition of the Blessed Sacrament, just look at Jesus in wonder and awe as Mary did, as any mother does at her child. That is prayer. That is silent adoration. That is contemplation.

You see, love is the sharing and from that act there is new life, new hope, new vision, new energy and new enthusiasm. If you want to get closer to Jesus, take your love and share it in a phone call, a card to the sick, a visit to the nursing home, hospitals or hospice. If you are seeking the face of Jesus and love, you will then find Him. Jesus and love are discovered in the sharing with the least of His children. That is where you give life and get life. One of the most difficult acts of love is to ask for forgiveness, right or wrong. This is a real miracle of grace. Life is too short to waste on negative feelings. Try to accept the outcasts of society, the addicts, the abortionists in your prayers. Jesus reached out to all and did not judge.

All of the above acts are the spirit of Christmas, of love, sharing and new life. Jesus did that His entire life. He loved, He accepted the poor, the down trodden, the leper, the disabled, the deaf and He gave them life. You are all called to walk in the steps of Jesus. This is the real spirit of Christmas. This is real gift giving. You will be amazed how the peace and love of Jesus fill you and your home.

⊕ **For your reflection:** *How have you attempted to put into practice, the teachings of Jesus? How have these attempts affected your spirituality?*

25. **Christmas Love II**

Love is dynamic and not static. In Christmas love there are three parts: Jesus, sharing and new life. Remember the Christmas story of Charlie Brown, which exemplifies love, the reality of life. The whole Peanuts gang is about to put on a Christmas play. Everyone gets a part. Charlie Brown is left out for there is no room for him. He is very disappointed and Lucy feels sorry for him. So she invites Charlie to be the director. He gets a big grin on his face and is proud that he has been chosen to direct the play. He tries hard but no one listens to him and Lucy has to help him. Finally he is commissioned to get a Christmas tree. He takes Linus and of course it is at the last moment. They look for a tree and can't find any decent tree. They finally pick a scraggly tree with few limbs and even some of them are bare. When Charlie arrives on the scene and shows the tree, the gang laughs at him, teases him and they walk away, disgusted at Charlie. This is another job he failed. Charlie walks home alone and in his misery.

In the meantime, Snoopy has been watching the scene. Snoopy then goes back to his dog house, which is all decorated. He takes the decorations from his house and puts them on the tree. The tree slowly takes shape and really looks beautiful. When the gang returns, they see this beautiful tree and they all praise Snoopy and Charlie. They sing and dance and the play is a great success.

This story has all the elements of true love. Snoopy in his love for Charlie, shares his own decorations. He proceeds to decorate the tree by himself. The gang, when they see the tree, now get new life for the play. That is life. That is love. That is Christmas love. This is the example that Jesus gives to you. Do things out of love. Share your own goodness with another. You give life but the other receives life. Tell others that you love them. Give a hug without looking for one. Ask for forgiveness. Life is short. Why live in past hurts when you can be healed and you can heal others. Share your toys, your charisma, your gifts from God.

God Our Loving Father sent His Son Jesus into the world to give you life and peace. He was born in love. Mary His Mother is the Mother of God. By that fact you became brothers and sisters of Jesus and you also became adopted children of God. Mary is your Mother. You have all the rights to the Heavens as His Son Jesus.

God loves everyone and you should try the same. There are many lost people in the world. There are the homeless, the disabled, those confined in nursing homes, many in jail, children caught up in drugs, addicts, girls seeking abortions. All of these are children of God. They are the gang. Many others have fallen through the cracks. They see no good in themselves and life. Even God seems to have abandoned them. You have the life. God needs you, His children, to reach out to His lost children. So at least pray for them and visit them and write them and call them. There are many things that can be done. Each is called to work in the Kingdom of God. You are all brothers and sisters in Christ. You are all children of God. So "love one another as I have loved you" is the gift of Jesus to you. That is Christmas Love.

May you all have a very Blessed and Holy Christmas and a Healthy New Year filled with the Blessings of God. You are worth it. Gifts are nice but "hugs" and a "I love you" are priceless.

Consider every morning you wake up, as a priceless gift of God. Every day is a new day and every day you have the choice of loving or not to love. You can make or break the day. What a gift from God!

✦ **For your reflection:** *How do you look at each day as you wake up? Is your love dynamic?*

26. **Why Are You Judge and Jury?**

You have seen, that you are a child of God. Jesus is the natural Son of God. Mary is the Mother of God. You are an adopted child of God. Mary is also your Mother. St. John writes, "You are children of God and have the special blessing of calling God "Father." Consequently you belong to the Kingdom of God with all the rights and blessings and privileges of a royal subject. Jesus said, "I do not consider you a slave but I now call you my FRIEND."

You have to believe in yourself, that you are a very beautiful and precious person. God did not make any junk. Be proud of who you are and how you look. God did not make any mistakes. If you believe anything is wrong with you, look at how you did it to yourself. If you do not like yourself, do not blame God. He created you in love and for love and to be free. Let's examine life's situations and examine what you may have done to cause you to be unhappy and lonesome and fearful.

Once you recognize that you are a child of God, your eyes are slowly opened to the reality of life. If you are a child of God with all the rights of the kingdom, then everyone else in creation is a child of God with the rights to the kingdom. For you are all created in the image and likeness of God. Consequently, God loves every creature with the same love that He gives and manifests to His Son Jesus. How can you be proud? What makes you believe that you are better than anyone else? Who has the audacity to judge another person? Why do you condemn others? What gives you the right to make others behave and act as you do? Who made you judge and jury? You frequently cannot decide what to do yourself. The old Indian saying that you cannot judge another person unless you walk in his moccasins is absolutely true. How do you know what is good or bad for your neighbor, when you frequently do not know what is good or bad for you? Did every decision in your life turn out just as you desired? Did you not make some mistakes? In your eyes it may appear bad but in the eyes of God, who knows? The merciful Lord can bring good out of everything as the Scriptures say.

Objectively, we say that the Twin Towers attack was wrong. Subjectively, in the eyes of the terrorists they believed they were doing the will of God. We saw it as wrong and rightly so, but in the hearts of the terrorists they believed they were right. How often has this happened to you? You say something or do something in all innocence. The other person takes it as a personal insult, or the outcome may have hurt someone. You believe that you are innocent and they believe that you are wrong. How many times have you been misjudged or misunderstood? Be honest. Why does your happiness and peace depend upon the actions of another? Why do wish to be in control of the other's life? You constantly push yourselves to succeed. You act to impress your neighbor. You never know or understand that you are a good person. You do not have to do anything to prove you are a good person. The above incidents are the reasons your lives are unhappy and not carefree and trusting as a child.

Being a child of God, you really never have to prove to anyone that you are a good person. The reason you can do good things, is because you are a good person. The thing you do is not what makes you a good person. The act is good, because you are good. When the tree is good, it will bear good fruit. All you have to do is play out your life by not hurting anyone or giving anyone any harm. No regrets. This allows you to be like a child in an adult world. You are free. There are no fears, anxieties, hurts, prejudices, only peace.

⊕ **For your reflection:** *How does, being a child of God, open your eyes to the realities of life and not illusions?*

Fr. John G. Sturm, S.J. - 1980

27. **Why Are You Judge and Jury? II**

You are in the Hands of God. He knows that what is happening world-wide is not His fault and He sees His children not acting in the way He created them. He does not enjoy it. He desires that someday they will come to their senses. When God saw what was taking place, He sent His Son to set things straight. "Reform your lives and listen to the good news" is the message of Jesus. You have the model in Jesus and you have the message of love and that is all that the Lord can do. He does not force anyone to follow Him. Thus it is difficult to understand the acts of others and it is more difficult to judge them. The Lord can draw good out of everything. It is not up to you to judge the world or any of God's children. All are in the Hands of the Lord. Everything is in the control of the Lord. Julian of Norwich, a woman mystic in the thirteenth century says, "All is well." Read carefully the following story and see yourself in it. I received it from Fr. Tony DeMello.

There is a Chinese story of a poor old farmer who had one horse for tilling his fields. One day the horse escaped into the hills and when all the farmer's neighbors sympathized with the old man over his bad luck, the farmer replied, "Bad luck? Good luck? Who knows?" A week later the horse re-turned with a herd of wild horses from the hills and this time the neighbors congratulated the farmer on his good luck. His reply was, "Good luck? Bad luck? Who knows?" Then, when the farmer's son was attempting to tame one of the wild horses, he fell off its back and broke his leg. Everyone thought this very bad luck. Not the farmer, whose only reaction was, "Bad luck? Good luck? Who knows?" Some weeks later the army marched into the village and conscripted every able-bodied youth they found there. When they saw the farmer's son with his broken leg, they let him off. Now was that good luck? Bad luck? Who knows? Everything that seems on the surface to be evil may be a good in disguise. And everything that seems good on the surface may really be an evil. So we are wise when we leave it to God to decide what is good luck and what bad, and thank Him that all things turn out for good with those who love Him.

There is a general principle of action, "Do not harm anyone and help those whom you can assist." This brings you a great light, peace and strength, which simplify life and brings common sense into making moral decisions. This principle satisfies most people, in day to day living. However, who decides what is "harm" and what is "help" for my neighbor in these circumstances? Who am I to do that anyway? If I can't decide things for myself, how can I decide what is good or bad for my neighbor? In all of this I have to follow my conscience and be aware of the common good.

The love of God is manifested in the love of the neighbor. You cannot harm anyone and should help others. This is a practical way of looking at the commandment of love. This frees you from deciding on reasons, frees you from scruples, frees you from details of legislation. Consequently you are not burdened with the responsibility of solving the problems of everybody or of the world. It is only up to you in the honesty of your conscience to be aware of the common good and to approximate the results. God will do the rest. God will change the bad into the good in His own way.

You do not know what is good or bad for anybody. But keep on doing cheerfully what seems to be most appropriate for this occasion. Do not have any weight or worry in your heart. You are in the hands of God, the world is in the hands of God. "All is well."

This should help you in the difficulty of gossip, of judging others, of jealousy, of holding grudges, of anger, of past hurts, of past sins. At any particular point in time everyone is a saint or sinner. Who knows? Sometimes in the course of life everyone is a sheep or goat. Love your neighbor in thought word and deed. Jesus loves you and He loves your neighbor.

✠ **For your reflection:** *How does the statement of Julian of Norwich "all is well" make you feel?*

28. **How to Change**

There are two necessary steps if you want to grow in the intimacy of the love of God. First, you have to admit that you have been wrong about your concepts of God and life. If you cannot see this, then these thoughts will not help you. The second step is to be willing to listen and to change. Personally, when I witnessed the growth and spirit filled faith of lay persons and priests, after Vatican II, I wanted a piece of the action. This is what happened to me. I then had to follow the two steps.

There has to be a willingness to unlearn the old and then learn the new. What was needed was an openness to the new. This was not easy. I had to reevaluate my spirituality. I felt very secure and did not want to change. It was necessary to put aside my objections and ideas and be ready and willing to listen. I had to unlearn many of my ideas and concepts of God. They did not fit the spirit of freedom which was expressed in the Council. I also noticed that there was a reawakening of the Holy Spirit throughout the whole world. This convinced me that God was at work in a new way. I also discovered, to my surprise, that I did not act any differently than my concepts of God. This statement absolutely amazed me. How does it affect you? When I examined the way I had lived, that statement was certainly correct. The renowned spiritual writer Thomas Merton said, that to grow in spirituality, is "the faith to unlearn our old tastes, feelings, ideas and concepts and begin to learn the right ones." Have you put yourself to the test? Are you willing to put yourself to the test? I did.

At a young age I learned that my idea about God was that I had to be obedient. I believed that He punished when I misbehaved and when I was good, He rewarded. I was wrong. God does not hand out rewards or bribe us. We cannot bribe the Lord. I tried and failed. I made a deal with Him. Canisius College offered me a football scholarship. The Holy Spirit was inviting me to the priesthood. There were many reasons I was avoiding the answer. Then I said to God "if I am injured I will quit playing football and my job at DuPont." During the summer I was hurt in an automobile accident. However, I said that I was not hurt on the football field and this does not count. I returned to school. The following year while playing football an injury took place. There was no way of backing down again. Then, the Jesuits picked up my option. Now, I share with you. You really cannot hide from the invitation and the love of God. Are your concepts of God any different today than they were when you were young? Why not? You are supposed to grow in wisdom, age and grace as Jesus did. This includes notions of God and your spirituality.

I had other ideas and concepts of God that were mistakes. To me God was in the distance. Sometimes He was the Judge, the All seeing Eye, a God with whom I believe I could bargain, or challenge. All of these were incorrect. I had to give up these ideas and relearn about God. These were my ideas. They were not God. God is different from your concepts and ideas. Do not substitute your ideas and concepts of God for God Himself. That is spiritual idolatry. The Love of God is unconditional. He is not a bookkeeper. There are no books in heaven as you have been led to believe. God does not live in the past. He does not remember the past. God is in the present. There is no past or future in the Lord. God lives in the present only. St. Paul gives a perfect description of God's love. Read one Corinthian 13, 4-15. Your mistaken attitudes direct and guide your entire lives and leave no room or time to enjoy life. Anxiety, worry, scruples, fear of dying and many other concepts hinder your growth in the love of God.

To grow in the love of God, you have to be willing to change, then you need the courage to go into action. You have to do it on your own. Do not worry about what others may think. You are different and it is your salvation. If something really disturbs you from the past, see the priest and clear the decks. Life is short and you are here to enjoy it.

Consequently, examine yourself about your ideas and concepts. If you have been mistaken, then admit it and be willing to change. As Jesus said "you cannot put new wine into old wineskins.".

Accept the invitation of Jesus to come and see. Find out what He has in store for you. Open the door to the mystery of your life. Wipe your feet on the mat and enter. Surprises await you. If you do not, you will never know. You really are on a gold mine.

⊕ **For your reflection:** *Why am I not willing to change? Am I perfect? A saint?*

29. Love of Self

How did you like the story of the horse and the old Chinese farmer? You are a child of God and believe that you are right. Your neighbor is a child of God and believes that he is right. Who knows? I remember telling others when I was a child that my Daddy was the best Daddy in the whole world. My friend would say, "My Daddy is the best in the whole world." Who was right? Both were right. Love is the acceptance of the other person. Love is destroyed and harmony does not exist and there isn't any peace when each person demands that he is right and the other wrong. You do not have to accept the actions of the other but it is necessary to accept the person. Jesus said, "Love the sinner and not the sin." He loved Peter but did not love the rejection. In John 8:2-8:11, there is the story of the woman caught in adultery. According to the law of Moses, such women had to be stoned. The Scribes said to him, "Teacher, this woman was caught in the very act of committing adultery. Now in the law, Moses commanded us to stone such women. So what do you say?" They said this to test him, so that they could have some charge to bring against him. Jesus bent down and began to write on the ground with his finger. But when they continued asking him, he straightened up and spoke. "Let the one among you who is without sin be the first to throw a stone at her." Again he bent down and wrote on the ground. And in response, they went away one by one, beginning with the elders. So he was left alone with the woman before him. Then Jesus straightened up and said to her, "Woman, where are they? Has no one condemned you?" She replied,

"No one, sir." Then Jesus said, "Neither do I condemn you. Go, (and) from now on do not sin any more." He did not even accuse her. He loved her and did not demand any conditions.

A basic law of relationship is treating others as you want to be treated. You will then live with very few regrets. All relationships of God and man begin with the love of self. You really need to love yourself. You need to know yourself intimately. What makes you click? What turns you on? What turns you off? How well do you know your physical body? What are your good qualities? What are your bad qualities?

You may discover that it is easier to find the bad qualities than the good. Why? That is a tough question and your spirituality, your relationship to God and others depends on your answer. Do you really love yourself? Give the reasons why or why not. The very famous question of Jesus was "Who do you say that I am?" You cannot answer that question unless you know who you are. How can you recognize goodness in your neighbor unless you can recognize goodness in yourself?

If you are serious about growing closer to the Lord and feeling more intimate, then you will take a sheet of paper and sit down and write the answers to the above questions. Be very specific in your answers and detailed. I think that you will be awakened to a deeper awareness of yourself and the presence of God in your life.

I have answered those questions a number of times on different occasions over the course of years. Every time the answers were a little different and I could see growth. Other people helped me to see qualities that I did not realize. Something we were taught when we first entered the Society of Jesus was to keep a daily diary of our prayer. Some days there was nothing to write and then on others my prayer unfolded. As you recheck your writings over time, you will clearly see how the Lord is leading and guiding you. Keep a diary.

Your body is a temple of God. It is the means by which you experience life. Your eyes, hands, feet, feelings, emotions, hearing, smells are the means by which you experience relationship to others and to creation and to God. The more you know about yourself the more you can appreciate yourself and others and the world.

✟ **For your reflection:** *Please sit down with pen and paper and write your answers to the many questions. See what happens? Writing does something to your spirit.*

30. **Love of Self II**

Your body is a gift of God to be loved and cared for and not mistreated. How much do you know about the gift of your body? For instance, as a little test, how big are your wrists? You see them every day. Can you describe your hands? Can you name and describe any of your feelings? Do you think everyone feels the same way? If you know so little about yourself, how can you dare to judge or condemn another? From grammar school on I liked my body, my height, my looks, my legs, my weight, my abilities, coordination and determination. I was very stubborn which put me into many scrapes. I was proud of my body and never smoked till I was 25. I kept in shape and outside of beer, I never drank any hard liquor. I was very successful in any sport. Studies suffered, I was poor in Latin and languages. I was never disheartened even though I could not understand how others could be achieving honors every marking period. I pedaled a bike 12 miles to and from school every day. Prayed as I rode and was faithful to the sacraments. Two of my favorite songs were "You've got to be a football hero to get along with the beautiful girls" and "A slow boat to China." I enjoyed life. I took piano lessons for two years and tap dancing for one. I liked music and dancing. I tried to develop the body God gave me, spiritually and physically. It was the only one I had. I was careful of what I ate. I wanted to be in good health. I did not smoke or get into serious trouble. Life to me was an opportunity to have fun, work, pray, study and enjoy the girls. The grace of God builds on nature. The graces you receive are built on your nature. How have you developed yourselves physically and spiritually? In general I liked that description of me. Now, you sit down and write about yourself beginning with your early school years.

To grow in spirituality and the love of God you have to know about yourself in detail. It is necessary to know your weak points and your strengths. How can you reject temptations, if you do not know your strengths? How can you fight against temptations, if you cannot detect the root of the difficulty? If you have a flat tire and fix it and then tomorrow another flat tire and fix it, you would do something about it. In the same way with temptations and weaknesses and anger, get to the root. To do this, you need to know all about yourself. When I entered the Society of Jesus, I was told to work on one temptation or weakness at a time to conquer it, rather than everything at once. You can do the same. It gives confidence in conquering temptations. Spend a week or more on each thing.

You have within you some things called passions and feelings. You do not see them but you sense them. They are manifested in your actions and reactions. The mystery of life is, they are least understood and yet are of vital importance in every facet of communication. When life goes on without them, it is cold and indifferent. When they are over emphasized, they are self-destructive. They are very delicate and need to be understood and accepted. How much do you know about your feelings? If you do not know your own feelings or understand them, how can you know and understand another person or situation? Yet you dare criticize, gossip, judge, are full of prejudices, condemn. You know that Jesus said, "before you do anything, first take the beam out of your own eye. If you have any thing against your neighbor, leave your gift at the altar, first make amends with your neighbor and then come to me."

⊕ **For your reflection:** *Describe who you are and not what you do.*

31. **Relationship**

Your body is a temple of God. It is holy by the fact that God the Holy Spirit dwells within you. It is the means by which you experience life in its fullness. Your eyes, your ears, your hands, your smell, your ears are the means by which you experience relationship to others, to God, to creation, to nature. The more you know about yourself, the more you can appreciate life, others and yourself. This awareness and action are in direct proportion to your love of God. Be aware that your body is a temple of God and it is the only life you have. Treat it with tender loving care and you will treat others the same way. Learn to love yourself. Avoid anything harmful to your health. God created you and you are unique. There is no one in this whole wide world who thinks like you, feels like you, loves like you. There is no one who can do the work for which God has created you. No one can take your place or fill your shoes. You alone have to give an account for your performance. You have been given life, a body, gifts, family, and these are your responsibilities. No one owes you a living.

Are you aware of what takes place within you in the course of a day, an hour, an incident? I certainly was not. On a retreat many years ago the priest said, "If the God you adore does not make you feel like a prince, then you are adoring the wrong God." From then on in I began to look at myself differently and tried to see how beautiful God made me. I started to look within myself and watch my reactions to life. Are you aware of what takes place in your life during the day? You know what you are doing, but are you aware of the sensations and feelings within you?

I always desired to feel peaceful, at ease, unruffled. When I was upset, mad, irritated and foolish, I really wanted to kick myself after the incident. How could I be so dumb as to have those negative feelings? When I realized what the negative feelings did to me, I had many regrets, for others must have also been hurt at that time. I tried to be decent, polite, thankful and respectful. The awareness of what took place in my life helped me to enjoy life more and others more.

Becoming aware of yourself is a wonderful way of overcoming temptations and addictions. When you begin to feel the negative sensations due to improper behavior, life will begin to change. Once you discover and are sensitive to your feelings, every moment of the day, you will notice a change in your person. In this awareness you will begin to love yourself more and reach out and feel more of the presence of God. Thus you will feel yourself being more accepting and forgiving. Your love pattern of life will become more vibrant. You will feel like a new person.

When you love yourself and respect your body and do not harm it, you love God. When you love and respect your neighbors and do not harm them, you love God in the same act. When you take care of the body God gave you and do not destroy it by drinking, smoking, drugs or any other bad behavior, you are loving yourself and God. When you eat properly, exercise, work and pray, you are loving God. When you do what is right to the best of your ability, you will be at peace. This is a sign of God's love for you. When you disrespect yourself or another or property, you are not loving yourself and not loving God.

When you are told to love yourself, try to understand what you have just read. The Holy Spirit will guide you and your common sense will direct you.

The purpose of life is to love. There is no way to love if you cannot appreciate your life or the life of another or creation. You first have to see goodness in yourself or goodness in creation, to love. You cannot give what you do not have. To show mercy, you have to be merciful. To give a hug, you need to know what it is to receive one.

For your reflection: *How do you rate your self-love on a scale of one to ten? Why?*

32. **Thoughts and Feelings**

You are created with body and soul. Your body is an integral necessity in your relationship to others and God. You are a beautiful temple. Each part of you is a delicate work of craftsmanship. God formed you and knew you while in the womb and watched you grow. You are specially loved and cared for. Consequently you should respect your body and not do anything to hurt it. Maintain good health and watch what you eat and drink. It is the only body you will ever have. You are responsible to God for it. It is like a precious and delicate gift of God. As you train your body, so you should develop your mind and spirit.

Your mind should be developed and trained. It gathers data and experiences of life and aids you in making decisions and enjoying life. It feeds on thoughts. You become the thinker. All the thoughts are your own. You create your own life style and are responsible for all you say and do. No one else can be blamed or praised for your actions. The abilities you possess cannot be given away. Your entire life is yours. It cannot be left behind. No one can improve on it.

Your thought system was developed by the past experience of life, your training, your culture. It contains all the information you have accumulated through the years. That is why you always act in a habitual manner. You developed it and formed it. But since you developed it you can change it. When something happens, you say, "Well, that is the way I am." That is true in a way, but you can change the way you live and act. You do not have to live in the past.

In your growth of the love of the Lord, many things may need to change to get rid of the baggage that you carry. You may say that is the way I am, but you do not have to remain that way. Take a good look at yourself and ask yourself, "Is this the way I am supposed to live?" Are other ways possible? Jesus is the way to the Father and some things have to be eliminated for you to feel closer and more intimate with the Lord. Those binds around your hearts, which prevent you from giving in to the will of the Lord, need to be eliminated. This is what Jesus means when He says that the person who loses his life will gain everlasting life. The same thing is true in marriage. It is necessary to change some things and attitudes but there is gained a new spirit of life.

I recall how my mind reacted when someone cut me off or blew his horn at a signal. My immediate reaction was irritation, to get even. The more I thought about it, the more irritated I became. I would then take steps to slow down at the signal or speed up to catch the person and cut him off. One day

I had a close call. I said, "Sturm, how dumb can you get? Let the guy go, you do not know him and he does not know you. He may have had a special reason for rushing." From that day on, I just let him go. I am more at peace. Others like that no longer have power over my actions.

When I think about life, I see that people are often like robots. You do the same things every day. You drive to work and return on the same roads. You always sit in a definite place in church. If someone tells you that you look fine, you beam. They tell you that you do not look good today, you go into a tizzy. You act and react always in the same way to certain remarks and criticisms. If others do not tell you that you are doing a good job, you are upset. Why? Did you ever try to analyze why you always react in the same way? Did you ever think that there may be a better way of living?

If you want to live in peace and to enjoy life, you have to understand your feelings. You cannot allow people to have power over you to make you happy or unhappy. You have to lead your own life. Do not depend upon another to fill your every need. No one can do that. You are the master of your own fate.

✠ **For your reflection:** *Consider your daily actions. Are you a robot or not?*

Fr. John and two special cousins - Jimmy and Nicky

33. **More Thoughts and Feelings**

Thoughts are the fathers of feelings. Every feeling comes as a result of a thought or thinking process or an outside reaction. Be aware of yourself and, in the course of the day, be sensitive to your feelings. If you feel distressed, you must have had some negative thoughts. If you feel jealous, it must come from jealous thinking. If you are unhappy, it is your negative thought about something. Just as you are responsible for your own thoughts, so you are responsible for your feelings. No one can make you feel sad and no one can make you feel happy. No one can make you feel guilty. No one can make you feel irritated. These feelings exist in you as all feelings do. You bring them upon yourself.

When you rise in the morning, you have a choice. You can choose to be happy or you can choose to be grumpy. It is your life. Think about this very carefully and try to understand. It is true for all of your feelings. You cannot blame anybody or anything for feeling the way you are. Let me repeat, you cannot blame anybody else or anything else for the way you feel. The feelings are in you. They are your feelings. No one causes them. Others may be the occasion, but they are not the cause.

The reason we are talking of thoughts and feelings is that they are the means you develop to arrive at a closer relationship to the one you love, to God and Jesus. St. Ignatius says to use the senses and imagination in prayer. God created you with a body and a spirit. In the manner in which your imagination, hands, eyes, ears, tastes, smells are how you experience life and love and relationship. You should use the same means to experience the love and the life of Jesus. The more that you can experience creation, nature, persons and life, the more you can feel and experience the love of Jesus. Just as in life, when you become more intimate with another, so you will become more intimate with Jesus. If you care, you can read the "The Song of Songs" in the Old Testament. It is a love poem about the love of God and His people. You will see in it the use of the imagination and all of the senses.

I will explain this idea of prayer as the opportunities arise. In the meantime, you need to become aware of your own person and its reactions to life. Sense the change that takes place within you during the day. In other words, become sensitive to your body and spirit. When you achieve this, prayer will take on a new meaning and the bible will come to life. Trust me. You have to allow the Holy Spirit to guide and fill you. You cannot do it by yourself. Right now, it is necessary for you to plant the seeds of awareness and let the Lord love you.

✠ **For your reflection:** *Do you realize that you are the cause of your own feelings? You cannot blame them on anyone else.*

34. **Imagination**

God gave you the gift of an imagination. Children know how to use it on their own. They have special friends, play games, become other people and pretend. You have an imagination and use it in day dreams, viewing the future, dreaming of what life could be like, day dreaming of the present or future. In prayer, put the gift of the imagination to work. You will be stunned by the insights you receive into the meaning of the prayer.

For instance, when you say the 'Hail Mary,' you are calling upon the Blessed Mother. When you call, she answers and appears before you. This is contained in the word "hail." You call her. She answers, "Here I am." You know her by name. She is delighted. It is like seeing a person and saying, "Hi Joe." He is delighted that you know his name. I remember meeting Bishop Mansell for the second time. When I met him, he called me by name. We had only met once, months before this occasion. I felt very good. When you say, "Hail Mary," she is delighted and is waiting upon you. What do you want? Say the prayer with fervor and really mean the words. You are praising her and begging her. I remember trying to obtain permission from my parents to play football. I pleaded, begged, washed the car, took out the garbage and even studied my homework. Finally they conceded. Prayer is the same way. Get a picture of whom you are praying to, be earnest, be serious, show that you are willing to sacrifice and do something. When you use your imagination and are sensitive to your feelings, your prayer takes on a richer and more intense appeal. It is better to say one Hail Mary with full attention than to rattle off a full rosary with no thought whatsoever. It is like reciting your grocery list to your next door neighbor. When you are finished, she really does not know what you want.

Use your imagination in every prayer. Can you picture Jesus when you are praying? What does He look like? What is the color of His eyes, hair, gown, sandals? Is He walking, sitting, praying, standing? Try to get an intimate picture. A photographer takes hundreds of pictures of a model. You should try your imagination in the same way with Jesus, the Angels, Theresa, Sr. Faustina and other saints. When you are praying, you do not actually recall all of these details. But the fact that your mind is now filled with a more detailed description, you are approaching prayer with a richer and a deeper knowledge. It fills you more as you pray and lessens the number of distractions. If you prepare, you do not wander off on wild journeys of thoughts and ideas.

When you say the "Our Father," you are talking to your Father. Get a picture in your mind, feel the respect within you. Remember that He loves you, He formed you, He knows you, He hands out gifts.

When you read the scriptures, picture the entire scene. The people involved, the conversation, Jesus, the crowds, the weather conditions, descriptions of the people involved; all of these elements need to be imagined. For instance, if you had a camera, how would you like to remember the scene? In this manner, try to imagine the scene in your prayer. The wedding feast of Cana should be easy to picture. You have all been to weddings. Put your imagination to work in prayer. You will experience a new enthusiasm in spirituality. In the spiritual exercises of St.Ignatius, the imagination is put to work. You are on safe grounds if you so pray. Try It.

✠ **For your reflection:** *Do you believe that you can develop this form of prayer? Why?*

35. Personal Feelings

Webster's definition of a feeling: a sensation, bodily consciousness, affection, emotion, passion. Some examples are: I am lonely or I feel lonely. I am happy, I feel happy, I feel sexy. I feel sad. I am cold. I feel gloomy.

The reason feelings are so important in life and in the spiritual life is, they are so personal. No one knows how you feel unless you tell and share it. I may be able to guess how you feel but it would be only a guess. Feelings are extremely private and very definitely private. Feelings are what separate you from the rest of the world. No two people feel the same in every way and in every circumstance. You are you, and that is the manner in which God created you.

Consequently it is impossible to imitate another in every degree. It is necessary to discover who you are and what makes you tick and what affects you. In what manner do you act and in what manner do you react. For instance, those of you who are married, what is your feeling when you can share with your husband and when you cannot? What are your reactions in the work force? You probably run a gauntlet of feelings. How do they affect you? You could probably get upset, loose your temper, get irritated, frustrated and many other feelings. How do you handle these situations?

If you could understand these feelings and situations, then you can take steps to maintain your peace and your common sense. Unless you understand your feelings, it is not possible to accept the other person or the situation. Once I understand feelings and what they do to me, then I can begin to understand how another acts. Therefore, I can have a more intimate relation with another and perhaps heal past hurts. This type of knowledge is invaluable in understanding the younger generation.

You know the second great commandment, "Love your neighbor as yourself." In order to love and understand your neighbor, you first have to love and understand yourself. The love of a neighbor and the love of God begin with the love of self. In fact, it is first necessary to love yourself, and then love your neighbor in order to love God. How does this make you feel?

In the course of the day, try to become aware of how you feel. What are the feelings? See how often they change. Try to understand how they affect you in your work and acting and talking. You will be amazed how little you know about yourself until you understand all of your feelings. Try to become aware of your whole person in the course of the day.

The second great commandment is, "Love your neighbor as yourself." How do you answer the question, do you love yourself? How does this make you feel? What have you done to yourself? God created the world and He created you in His own image and likeness. When He created you, you were good. In searching out your own feelings, you will begin to see your own goodness.

The marriage encounter weekend was based on feelings. It was then and through the years of sharing about feelings, I experienced my own goodness and the beauty of God's creation and His creatures.

Men and women have feelings. You have experienced them, but frequently you do not recognize their value in relationship. When God said to love one another, He did not exclude feelings. It is necessary to admit to them and to recognize them.

✠ **For your reflection:** *For your reflection: For instance, can you admit to a feeling, recognize it and share it?*

36. **My Feelings**

The present chapter presupposes the former chapter. The reason you need to know and express your feelings will become more obvious. Jesus was not only Divine, but also Human. Consequently, He was like us. He had feelings, affections, passions and so on. In your struggle to obtain a more intimate relationship with Jesus, you need to know your feelings in order to get an idea of how He feels about you. The first commandment, Mt. 12:30 "You shall love the Lord your God with all your heart, with all your soul, with all your mind, and with all your strength." The second is "You shall love your neighbor as yourself." There is no other commandment greater than these. Thus, intimacy and closeness depend on the knowledge and love of yourself. The manner in which you experience relationship in life will give you a tiny sense of God's love, compassion, forgiveness and sacrifices for you. How you feel about God and how you experience His love depends on how you experience the love and compassion and forgiveness of your neighbor. You cannot experience more love of God than you have for your neighbor. That is the test and thermometer. The love of your neighbor is the measure of your love of God.

A feeling is not a thought, nor an attitude, nor is it love. Love is an act of the will. It does not depend on feelings. It is great to have positive feelings as they make love easier. But there are days and weeks when the feelings are not so nice and yet there still is love. Love is a decision.

A feeling is not a thought or an attitude. Feelings are expressed by the words, I am tired, I am lonely, I am depressed, I feel lonely, I feel cold, I feel upset. Read this carefully. If I say, "I feel that you are driving too fast," this is not a feeling. When you add the word "that" after the word "feel," you have a thought. I could just as easily say, "I think that you are driving too fast." This statement can be argued because it is an opinion. If I said, "I am nervous the way you are driving," then this statement cannot be argued. You may never argue about a feeling because feelings are neither right nor wrong. They just are.

Just listen to talk shows. The word "feel" is constantly used in the wrong sense. They will ask, "how do you feel about the East situation?" Then someone will say, "I feel that there will be lots of trouble." This is a thought and not a feeling. The word "that" was used after the word "feel."

Look at yourself and try to sense how you feel while you are doing something, or saying something, or praying, or going to church, shopping and so on. You have many feelings. Can you even name them? Describe them? In attempting to become of aware of your feelings, stop now and then through the day and ask yourself, "How am I feeling?" As the days go on, you will become very sensitive to your person. It will aid you in taking better care of yourself.

It will make you more sensitive to the needs of your own body, your spirit and your peace of mind. It will draw you closer to your family, neighbors and the Lord. In another way, it will help you to avoid temptation because you will experience what happens inside your conscience. You will experience less guilt if you become more aware of yourself.

✟ **For your reflection:** *Do you see or believe that in attempting to experience your feelings, that this will help you grow spiritually?*

37. My Feelings

You are created in the image and likeness of God. God has created you a sensual person, filled with all types of feelings. It is necessary to understand this, for the feelings are a part of you. Some feelings need to be expressed. To discover the beauty of a feeling, you need to recognize it and try to describe it. It is possible to go through life by denying feelings. However if you deny them, you are not fully human. You hurt yourself and everyone else around you. You are a cold person, an unfeeling person.

The feeling of grief, if not shared, can slowly destroy your happiness. It may even be the source of ill health. The feeling of grief can be so deep that it controls your whole life. You will never be happy and reconciliation with the Lord is difficult. It needs to be shared. Living on past hurt feelings will never bring you peace and happiness. This is not the way to God.

Feelings are very personal and no two persons feel alike. If you do not understand this, then dialogue and communication and sharing are impossible. You may persuade another to think as you do, but you can never make another to feel as you do. The phrase, "I know how you feel" is inaccurate.

The Sturm Family

You may guess but you really do not know. You will never know how another person feels until the other person tells you and describes it. When you can give a description of a feeling, you are beginning to become aware of whom you are.

In order to intimately love another or Jesus, it is necessary to know and experience your feelings. If you tell Jesus that you love Him what goes on within you? Are they just words? The words only manifest your thought. Feelings express your heart. If you share with another "I love you" in a sort of casual or customary word, it is cold and impersonal. If it is said with the heart and feelings, there is warmth and it is personal. You know this and know the difference.

Just analyze yourself in what you say and do and see how you feel. When you become aware of yourself in this fashion, you will discover a beautiful gift, namely yourself.

Discovering your feelings is a grace of God to aid you in conquering temptations. If you are given to loss of temper, feelings run high. A short time later you could kick yourself. When you realize your feelings and how you hurt yourself, it will dawn on you that you are the loser. Just look at yourself in any temptation. Become aware of all those feelings inside of you. This will aid you in conquering temptations. To understand your feelings is the best way to avoid temptations.

Once you begin to discover the beauty of yourself and share those feelings, you will draw closer to the Lord. You are created in the image and likeness of God. Jesus was filled with feelings. To understand Jesus you need to understand your own feelings. If you feel compassion, you get a sense of how Jesus did when He had compassion on the multitude.

You will grow deeper in love with the Blessed Mother. She was a woman with a human heart. Devotion to the Blessed Mother, and observing her taking care of Jesus and Joseph and her home, should arouse many of your own feelings. Imagine the Blessed Mother and picture her in her daily actions. This is a form of prayer.

Feelings are gifts from God. There is nothing wrong with them. They help describe who you are. They are neither good nor bad. They merely exist. There is no morality to a feeling. You cannot go to hell for feelings alone. They are part and parcel of human nature. Everybody has feelings. Jesus was filled with feelings.

⊕ **For your reflection:** *Did you ever stop to think about the importance of sharing feelings in relationship and prayer?*

38. **More Feelings**

There isn't any morality to a feeling. It just exists. Feelings are like clouds that come and go. Some are dark and foreboding. Others are bright and cheerful. Feelings do not last and can change in an instant. You can go from feeling hot to cold in moments, from happiness to fear in a phone call. A messenger at the door can bring fear. Everyone has feelings. Women are ready to talk about them, while men are frequently fearful of admitting their existence. It is the modern world's idea of weakness that men should not cry and that they should bury the feelings.

Feelings are not sinful. You are created as a sexual and sensual person. These are not sinful. You cannot go to purgatory or hell for feelings. Feelings do not become sinful. If you act on them, the act becomes sinful to some degree. The feeling does not become sinful. If you feel hatred for some one and then act upon it, you are wrong. If you continue to harbor the feeling of hate and feed on it and keep it as part of your life, your way of life becomes sinful.

Feelings describe your person. The feelings are not you. They are what dress you up. You are always the same, but the feelings come and go. It is similar to changing clothes or getting a new hair style. The change of clothes is not you, nor is the hair style.

People are known by their feelings. Some people are kind, cold, selfish, proud, humble, generous, lonely, and so on. How do you describe yourself in terms of feelings? If you say that you do not have any, then you are calling God a liar. Everyone has feelings. You are made in the image of God.

How do you explain your life in terms of the second great commandment? You are to love your neighbor as yourself. If you do not recognize your own self worth, your feelings, your needs, how are you going to love your neighbor?

If you do not feel mercy, and have not experienced it, how are you going to be merciful to your neighbor? How about forgiveness? If you have not forgiven yourself or been forgiven, how are you going to forgive another? If you do not sense being needful in life, how are you going to sense the need of another? All, all, all spiritual growth in life begins in you. If you do not recognize this, you will never achieve the peace and joy and love that God has in store for you from the very beginning. No one can give you spirituality. You have to work for it.

Discovering your own feelings, admitting to them and sharing them is like finding diamonds or pearls. You now begin to recognize that you are really a temple of God. Just like the scriptures describe, you are like a bride adorned with diamonds and gold. You see yourself as beautiful as a bride of Christ. You are really a princess. You are created with the loving hands of a Loving Father.

Being able to recognize your own feelings is essential to communication and dialogue. How can you communicate with another if you haven't any knowledge of your own feelings? How can you pray? Jesus went off by Himself to pray. He was interrupted. When He saw the crowd, He had compassion on them. He felt sorry for them. He felt something and then He did something about it. In like manner, you are to be aware of your feelings and then share them. Be open to God and neighbor.

✢ **For your reflection:** *Did it ever dawn on you that there is more to life than meets the eye? Why not reach out and try the above suggestions?*

39. **Feelings Described**

As you have read, feelings are neither right nor wrong. They merely exist. The feelings are not you. The feelings only describe you. They are fleeting like the clouds. They come and go. Some clouds are fluffy and white, others thick and dark, some are gloomy and eerie. Behind all the clouds is a very beautiful blue and sunny sky. It is the same with you. You are a beautiful person and the clouds only describe what is going on within you at that time. The feeling does not last. It is necessary to remember this.

The more you become aware of your feelings and what they do to you, the easier it is to understand temptations and to conquer them. Once you begin to understand yourself, you gain a sense of freedom as a child of God. The freedom will feel like a heavy burden lifted from your shoulders. Guilt disappears in many cases. Scruples begin to come under control. You feel more confident.

To know yourself is necessary for communication and dialogue. This is needed in all walks of life, at home, with your children or at work. Become aware of your own feelings and what they do to you. At the same time, understand that no two persons feel alike. Each is unique. Consequently, no two people react alike in any given situation. How often have you said to yourself that you would not act in the same manner as someone else? So you get upset. Why? People are different. When you understand what happens to you, you will become less frustrated, annoyed, upset and so on about some other person or incident. People are different, cultures are different, and status in the community is different. Why presuppose that everybody should act like you?

There are many feelings and it is always interesting when you discover them. Then it is mind blowing to be able to describe them. You will then begin to understand how other people may feel.

For instance, the other day I was picked up for lunch. The person who drove me made a turn going the wrong way on a one- way street. I felt very embarrassed. In a second, it turned to fear and anxiety for a car was heading in our direction. So when you have a situation in which you feel embarrassed, you may describe it as, "embarrassed like driving down a one way street." I know what that means and helps me to understand you better.

You may say: I feel contented like relaxing in the sunshine; I feel annoyed as having a chipped nail; I feel honored like being invited as a special guest; I feel lonely like entering a room where I do not know anyone; I feel shocked like touching a live wire; I feel satisfied like baking a delicious pie; I feel impatient like waiting for someone who is late; I feel elated like winning the office pool; I feel fortunate like having a bad golf shot turn out fine; I feel anxious like waiting in a doctor's office; I feel refreshed like having a beer on a hot day; I feel guilty like not responding to an invitation; I feel excited like getting my first date; I feel very sensual when walking barefoot in the wet grass; I felt thrilled when my cataracts were removed successfully. Use your imagination. You can do it if I can.

Jesus spoke in this manner. When asked about the Kingdom of Heaven he said, "It is like a woman in search of her pearl and when she finds it she calls in her neighbor. The Kingdom is like a King who invites guests to a wedding feast. When you pray, do not be like a hypocrite. Jesus had pity on them, for they were like sheep without a shepherd." There are 223 passages in the New Testament, which use the word "like." I find it very interesting to try to describe my feelings. I also enjoy others who describe their feelings. Listening to others helps me to discover more about my own feelings. When the feelings are described, it shows how beautifully the Lord has made everyone without exception.

Try it and see what happens. It will also deepen your prayer life.

✛ **For your reflection:** *Use your imagination and try to describe your feelings.*

40. **Feelings for Communication**

Jesus often spoke in descriptive terms. He did this so that you could more clearly understand His message. There are 91 uses of the word "like" in the Gospels. "Like" is used 132 times in the remaining books of the New Testament. The word "like" is used 1083 times in the Old Testament. When something is described, it becomes clearer. For instance, when you say you are feeling "good," can you describe how it feels? When you say that you are feeling good, I know what it does not mean, but I really do not know what it means to you, unless you can describe it.

When you are sad, what is it like? What does it feel like when you are feeling "used?" Is it a feeling of being a door mat? Or what? What is the feeling when someone cuts you off in driving? Or blows their horn at a signal? What are your feelings when you pass an accident on the road? How does the feeling of embarrassment touch you? What are your feelings when you meet a handsome man or a beautiful woman? You are filled with all kinds of feelings. When you can discover them and describe them you are advancing in the personal love of the Lord. How do you feel when your children say, "I hate you?" Describe it. When you can describe your own feelings, it gives you a deeper sense of relationship. The recognition of your feelings makes you more aware of yourself, neighbor and God.

Feelings run deep and they vary in intensity. Each feeling has its effects upon a person. They are not the same for each person.

You are made in God's image and likeness. For instance, gratitude must fill your hearts as you feel and see your children or grandchildren act in the way you have taught them. Jesus feels the same about you.

Feelings are neither right nor wrong. Some are positive and some negative. None of those feelings are sinful. The sin comes on acting upon them. NO ONE GIVES YOU THESE FEELINGS. All of those feelings are yours. Those feelings are your reactions to life. You are responsible for any action you take as a result of your feelings. The more you appreciate your feelings and accept them, the happier and freer you will be. Jesus said, "I have come to set you free that my joy may be in you."

Other things and persons are the occasions of your feelings, but they do not give them to you. Your feelings belong to you. When you were little and bumped your head upon the table, your Mother may have said, "you nasty table." The table did not feel any pain. The same is true of all the occasions of your feelings. Everyone does not feel the same as you. If you have experienced the boat ride at Niagara Falls, everyone will come away with different feelings. Niagara Falls did not give you the feelings. It was only the occasion of them. Some people cry at a movie. Other people do not. The movie was the occasion of the tears, but not the cause of them. If the movie was the cause of tears, everybody would have tears. You are the cause of all your feelings.

Take a few minutes and think about you being the cause of all your feelings. You cannot blame anyone for being bored. You cannot accuse anything or anyone for feeling unhappy. You cannot blame anyone or anything or any event for being lonely. You cannot blame anyone for being angry. Pray that you can understand this and you will begin to feel the freedom and the joy that Jesus came to share with you.

Become aware of yourself as the day goes on. See if you can discover how the feelings work in you. Try to understand what feelings do to you. Once you begin to understand what the feelings do to you, you will be happier.

✠ **For your reflection:** *What is your opinion of the statement that you are the cause of all your feelings.*

Prefect of Discipline - Canisius High School 1952-1970

41. **Feelings of Illusion**

If you feel anger and blame the other person, you are living an illusion. The other person did not cause the anger. He was the occasion of the anger, but he was not the cause of the anger. You are wasting your time and not enjoying life. Don't you see that the other person has power over you? The other person could have been the occasion, but they were not the cause of your anger. The feeling of anger was your personal reaction to the incident. The anger is in you. As long as you are angry, you are in the power of the other person. She has control of you. You now lead your life with the anger directing your every move and thought. You are living in the past.

The same is true when you react negatively to someone who cuts you off while driving. If you get upset, mad, irritated, agitated or cranky, it is your fault. The other guy goes blissfully on his way. He has power over you. If you think that you are an independent thinker and no one can tell you what to do, then look at your feelings and watch your reactions to life. You are not as independent as you think.

Feelings such as anger and grief need to be shared, otherwise they can fester. Sooner or later they will come out and hurt you and even cause sickness. Your whole life and decisions are guided by their insidious effects. By the time you realize it, life is over. You cannot run from yourself or life. You were created to love. If you are driven by hate or anger, you are working against your own nature. That is why you should have a good friend in whom you can confide. Do not let personal pride slowly destroy your life. You only have one life and there are no repeats. This is it. Life is not a dress rehearsal.

Try to look at your reactions to things and persons during the day. Be aware of the feelings. How would you describe it to another? When you read, are you aware of how the author describes situations and the persons?

You may describe feelings with degrees of intensity by using numbers from one to ten. Feelings can be described by using colors, incidents from your experiences of life, common experiences, children, vacations, work and the like. It is necessary to use your imagination. The question is: what is the feeling like? Try to describe it.

For me, writing these articles is like revealing secrets to friends. I feel honored, like being chosen to sit at the head table of a wedding. It makes me feel warm all over. When someone says they enjoy the articles in the bulletin, I beam like the sun coming through varied colored windows.

I will give you lists of feeling words. The following are "happy" words. Then, you have to learn how to describe them.

Agreeable	Delightful	Good	Joyous
Blissful	Enthusiastic	Grateful	Lovable
Bubbly	Fantastic	Gratified	Loved
Cheerful	Fortunate	Great	Loving
Cheery	Funny	Heavenly	Lucky
Contented	Generous	High	Warm
Delighted	Glad	Joyful	Over-joyed
Pleasant	Pleased	Satisfied	Wonderful

Begin to enjoy yourselves and life. Life is short. As one spiritual writer said, "Lose your mind and come to your senses." Take time out to smell the roses, walk barefoot in the dewy grass, take a walk in the park, enjoy a trip to Letchworth Park in the fall, look at the trees and the varied colors of the leaves. Did you know that it would take a lifetime to find the essence of a fly? Look up at the moon and the sky. Creation is beautiful and God has given it to you to enjoy. Welcome your feelings before it is too late to enjoy the gifts of God.

✚ **For your reflection:** *What is time and how does it make you feel?*

42. **Negative Feelings**

Feelings are either positive or negative. The positive feelings are usually enjoyed, but there is not much personal learning experience in them. When you are feeling good, you are not tested in any way. Everything is fine. There are real benefits and very special graces in negative feelings. These manifest the very same areas that have not as yet been redeemed. You have been created to be in peace and harmony with yourself. A negative feeling tells you that you need to rid yourself of something or a way of acting. For instance, if someone disturbs you, that is probably the same thing in you that you do not like about yourself. If another person disturbs you, it is usually the very same thing in you which disturbs someone else. If you do not like an action of another, then take a good look at your own actions. You will find that your actions are of the same kind. If you are jealous of another, remember that the jealousy is in you. The other person is not the cause, only the occasion. Negative feelings usually manifest that you live in the power and the control of another. You react and think and judge according to these negative feelings.

When you become aware of what negative feelings do to you, you will see how they hurt you. Then you will begin to act differently and pray differently and not be disturbed. You will live in peace as Jesus desires. You will no longer judge another, you will be more tolerant, and you will be willing to change and to listen better. You will no longer play god over another. Everyone was created beautifully and there is good in everyone. If God does not judge or condemn, then how can you?

I remember when I joined Marriage Encounter, Father Frank was quoted very frequently and people praised him for his way of talking and sharing. I was sort of jealous, for I did not hear anything like that about my weekends. I would have liked that sort of adulation. I then tried to imitate Fr. Frank and say the same things. It did not work. I learned the hard way. I had to be myself and share my feelings, and it worked like a charm.

The same for you. Do not imitate, judge, condemn or be jealous. You are just as beautiful as another, if you look into yourself and see your charms and blessings. God loves you in the same way as He loves any other person. Trust in your own goodness and trust in God Who created you.

In the final analysis, does it make any difference what another person thinks of you? It is your relationship to God that is important. What others think of you does not influence God in any way. Treat others and think of others in the same way that you wish to be remembered. When you discover a negative feeling, do not blame another. It is a grace of God to look into yourself and to see what is causing this feeling. God always brings good out of what you consider bad. Frequently what you consider one of your best points is the occasion of a negative feeling in another. Take a good look at yourself and your relationship to your spouse. No one is perfect. You are not the last word.

When a negative feeling arises, it is a grace and a gift from God to look into yourself and see what is wrong. It really is an invitation from God to better yourself. Do not blame another and do not blame the past or present circumstances. The feelings are in you and not in another.

Here are some more feeling words to ponder.

Angry	Annoyed	Bitter	Boiling
Enraged	Exasperated	Fed up	Furious
Grouchy	Indignant	Inflamed	Revengeful
Infuriated	Irked	Outraged	Quarrelsome
Rage	Red-hot	Seething	Displeased
Disturbed	Worked up	Mad	Violent

To understand more about the love and mercy of Jesus, it is necessary to know and experience your own feelings. If you can experience yourself and if you feel compassion, you will begin to experience the love and mercy and compassion of Jesus. You cannot give or share what you do not have or recognize.

✠ **For your reflection:** *Has reading and thinking about feelings influenced your way of life? How?*

43. **Interpretation Feelings**

Feelings are not you. The feelings are like clouds; they come and go. You remain the same. When you fly, you frequently go through a cloud level. Above the clouds is the sun. Feelings are the same in you. They describe what is going on in you, but they are not your real self. You are like the sun. You are above the feelings. Feelings come and go, but you remain.

When others judge you, they are not judging you, but judging the way you act or perform. You are not the acting or the performance. The actions are seen by others. When you identify yourself with your work or acts, then you will get hurt. When you believe that someone who criticizes your work is criticizing you, you are identifying yourself with your work and you will get hurt. The feelings are in you, but they only describe how you feel. You are not your feelings. Your feelings are not you and your actions are not you. You remain the same, but the feelings change. It is similar to changing clothes. You are not your work. The work can be destroyed, but you remain. You are not a doctor, but being a doctor is what you do. You are not a housewife, but being a housewife is what you do. For instance, when someone criticizes you, you can get a fit of anger. Why? They are not criticizing you, but what you may have said or done or are wearing. Why get angry? Why allow others to have power over you? If someone says you have a nice hair style, you feel great. In this way you are like a robot. Someone says a good thing and you feel good. Then someone says something bad and you feel bad. In this way of reacting, you are saying that your happiness depends on someone or something outside of you. That is really living an illusion. Real happiness exists in you. Happiness does not depend on your hair style. If they like it, fine. If they do not like it, fine.

The negative feelings are the most difficult. You have your own negative feelings as a result of something you do or said. Then there are negative feelings about something or someone. It is necessary to understand your feelings and how to handle them. Feelings, such as anger, guilt, sadness, hopelessness or grief, take their toll in your way of life. It takes your human nature quite some time to readjust your life style. Those feelings need to be understood, so that you can let them pass and work through you. As long as they exist, they rule your life. God does not desire you to live in the past. He is not in the past and He desires you to be with Him on a day-to-day basis. It is not Christian to live in the past. It is not living a life of faith.

"I am annoyed," "I am fed up." "I am disappointed," "I am not angry, but I am close to it," "I am angry" or "I am mad" are all forms of anger. S ome times you are quick to anger.

Sometimes it takes a long time. You take a slow boil. All of these feelings are in you and they are your feelings. You have to learn how to avoid getting angry.

Use the feeling of anger to warn you to reexamine your thinking. Get rid of your prejudices. When you are contradicted, you are usually prejudiced. It manifests to you that you are not listening to the other. Take a deep breath and try not to allow the situation to get to you. Identify situations in which you are liable to get angry. Know how to avoid them. Make mental notes of incidents in which you get angry and try to have a more positive attitude. Do not allow people to get control of you.

In certain cases, it is necessary to ask for forgiveness. For this you will need prayer and the grace of God. Do not let pride get in your way of loving God.

If you have a quick temper, then it is up to you to look deep within you. Why is it necessary that you always be right, or that you have your own way? What is in you that flares up instantly? You are the cause of your own instant anger.

Anger can get you sick, raise your blood pressure, live in frustration, say and do things that you will regret or cause bodily injury. Anger is something everyone needs to tame.

Here are some more feeling words. Learn your own feelings to grow in the personal love of God and the wonderful way the Lord has formed you.

Afraid	Anxious	Alarmed	Apprehensive
Fear	Frozen	Horrible	Pale
Panicky	Paralyzed	Scared	Shy
Terrified	Threatened	Timid	Jumpy
Dreadful	Jumpy	Distrustful	Horrified

The grace of God builds on nature. The more you rid yourself of the negative, the more you grow in perfection and the grace of the Lord. All feelings are inside you. You developed them, and therefore you can eliminate them or control them. Ask the Holy Spirit to guide you. You cannot do it by yourself. Common sense is your best offense against the feelings ruling you.

✟ **For your reflection:** *What does the phrase, "grace builds on nature," mean to you?*

44. Grief

Grief is another feeling. Grief is not you. It is a feeling. However, it cannot be protected by you. If it is concealed and not expressed, it slowly festers inside you and eats its way like a cancer. It affects your thoughts, your way of acting and also your loving. It is really another form of self-pity. You may believe that as long as you are grieving, you are loving. If you stop grieving, then you believe that you no longer love that person. You are not really grieving for the lost person. How can you grieve for a person who is perfectly happy in heaven? Are you so selfish that you want that person back with you? That is not love; that is possession. If you try to possess a person, that is not love; that is a form of slavery. Love means that you are free and the person is free.

Prolonged grief is really self-pity. You are saying to God, "Why have you done this to me?" Then the rest of your life is governed by grief. You live in grief, you eat in grief, you sleep in grief, you love in grief, and you die in grief. All of this is in vain. It is really another form of vanity. It is bad grief.

Charlie Brown has a pet phrase, "Good Grief." There is good grief and bad grief. Good grief comes as a result of someone who is really loved. The more you love, the greater the grief. The good grief aids you in the separation. In faith, it gives you a deeper sense that you are in the hands of the Lord. It is a part of God's way of loving His creatures. It takes some time for the heart to heal and to readjust to the separation. The heart is capable of great love in all circumstances and can learn to adapt itself to life. There is a reasonable time in the life of a Christian to grieve. Then life has to take over. You are all children of life. Life is in the present and not in the past. Living in grief for a very long time is living in the past. God is not in the past. It is not Christian.

Fr. John and the baptism of his niece

I remember when my Dad died. Every night my Mother went to her room and cried. Tears are gifts from the Holy Spirit and are for cleansing. Never suppress tears in yourself or another. I asked my Grandmother if I should go back and talk to her. Gramma said, "No, let her alone." This went on for about three weeks. After that my Mother told us, "I have to get on with my life." The extended crying period was over. She loved my Father, she missed my Father; yet she began to come alive. The grief had not ended, but now Mother was better adjusted to get along with her life.

Parents, who have lost a child, never get over their grief. However, there are ways of communicating and sharing with others to help you get through the grief. Grief cannot be kept a secret within you. It needs to be shared to be healed. The healing takes place in the sharing of the grief. It cannot be healed by keeping it a dark secret inside you. If this concerns you, read the book "A Grief Observed" by C. S. Lewis. Getting over grief does not mean that you no longer love. It awakens you to a new set of values and the love of God. When you work your way through it, you now control it and it no longer controls you.

I'll tell you a story of a family and the sudden loss of a two-year old baby. It was their first child. When the baby died, and after the ceremony, I took the baby to the cemetery. The parents were destroyed. They gave away all of the child's things, sold the house and moved. They began a group of parents who lost children. Weekly, and with supervision, they shared their problems and grief. Their lives changed. One time they asked me, "How is it you do not ask about our son?" I said that I was afraid that it may bring back sad memories. "Oh no," they said, "it shows us that you still remember him."

Every person has to learn how to handle their feelings. You can learn much from others in the same set of circumstances. Do not go through life living in the past. You will never be happy. God and happiness are not in the past but in the present. Pray that your feelings may be healed.

More feeling words:

Weak	Burdened	Coming-apart	Debilitated
Helpless	Lazy	Defensive	Destroyed
Drained	Exhausted	Frail	Overcome
Powerless	Shattered	Spent	Inadequate

It is good to know some of the names of feelings. It will aid you in attempting to describe them. It is in the description of what the feeling does to you that you can arrive at some ways of handling them. This will help you to understand them. In this manner, you will begin to find peace.

✟ **For your reflection:** *Grief can overcome you in many forms of separation. There is grief over divorce, death of an animal, separation from a close friend, children gone astray. How do you handle grief?*

45. Good Grief

I remember when my Father died. I had just left home for the priesthood. I was gone about a year. I returned for the funeral and remained home about three weeks with my Mother. The Society of Jesus asked my Mother if she needed me at home. If so, I could stay. My Mother refused and she said, "I would rather scrub floors than allow John to come home to support me." My grandmother lived with us, and passed away a year later. My sister entered the convent. My brother had to join the army. This all happened within a year. My Mother was left alone in a big house. Every person has to face grief in one form or another. How much are you willing to give up, sacrifice, in order to work through your grief and get on with your life? This is the test of firm faith and true love. There is a time to grieve and then a time to live.

I remember when my Mother died. I walked around as if in a daze. Life seemed so different. I went through the motions, but there did not seem to be any life. All the things that I thought would happen never came up. All the feelings I thought would be involved, did not affect me. Nothing, of which I had anticipated, occurred. It seems God had it all planned to fit me. It took about six months to work through that period. Thanks be to God that

I had my Jesuit community to support me and listen. What a blessing!

Grief has to be worked through. It takes time to face the new reality. The heart has to adjust to the separation.

There are four like stages:

1. **Shock vs. Reality:** The task of this stage is to accept the reality of the loss. The person is gone and will not return. You will be in a state of shock.

2. **Protest vs. Experience:** The task is to experience the pain of grief rather than suppress or avoid it. You need to face the pain of loss, feel the pain, and express your pain rather than run away from it. The longer you supress it, the longer the pain and grief will remain. It will affect your whole life.

3. **Disorganization vs. Adjustment:** You have to adapt to your new ways of living without a spouse, coming to terms with living alone, raising children alone, facing an empty house, managing finances and taking on new roles.

4. **Attachment vs. Reorganization:** Detaching from the person, memories and hopes and reinvesting in other relationships or in a job. Life does not wait for you. When you face a loss with God's help and y our hope in Christ your Savior, while experiencing the feelings and hurts of grief, you are promoting healing. Jesus said, "Come to me all you who labor and are burdened and I will refresh you."

This period tries your faith, but it is a time to grow in the trust of the Lord and recognize how you are totally dependent on God. It also aids you in feeling the great separation when the Lord calls you. He will lead you into the heavenly paradise. Everything is left behind. Those in heaven are in perfect peace and happiness. Their love for you is to enjoy life and find peace and happiness. They do not wish you to be unhappy or waste your life on what has been. You can pray to them to help you. They are great intercessors before the throne of heaven. In their love for you, they will protect you and aid you in all your needs. Learn to trust in the Lord. If you care to visit the cemetery, fine. However, do not make those visits the center of your new life.

These are some SAD feelings:

Awful	Blue	Brokenhearted	Dejected
Despairing	Distressed	Down cast	Gloomy
Grim	Hopeless	Ignored	Melancholy
Low	Joyless	Left out	Lonely
Grief-stricken	Dependent	Mean	Melancholy
Pensive	Rotten	Imposed-upon	Sorrowful
Weepy	Woeful	Overburdened	Solemn
Agony	Confused	Crushed	Miserable

Once you recognize the feeling, it gives a sense of relief. You know that it will pass. Now it is up to you to accept it in such a way as to give you inner peace. In the meantime, pray. The Lord loves you.

✟ **For your reflection:** *When it comes to faith do you really believe in the words of the Lord, "In my Father's house there are many mansions?" He has also told you that He loves you. He said in John 14:3, "If I go and prepare a place for you, I will come back again and take you with me, so that where I am you also may be." That is real love.*

46. **Fear**

You are filled with many types of fear. You know this from your own experience in life. There are those who say that there are only two things in life, God and fear, or love and fear.

Fear is the cause and the root of all the evil in the world and all the hurts. I do not think that there is any evil in the world that is not caused by fear of some sort. The truly nonviolent person is the one who is fearless. Take a look at yourself. It is only when you are afraid that you become angry. Try to remember the last time you were angry and search for the fear behind it. What were you afraid of losing? What were you afraid would be taken from you? Were you afraid of losing self-respect? Power? Prestige? See the fears inside of you and you will sense the cause of your anger.

When you see angry persons, try to analyze how frightened they are. Ultimately there are only two things, love and fear.

The young and the old have fears. As you get older there is a fear of outgrowing your usefulness. You may believe that God and others are losing interest in you and you no longer have any purpose. This is really a deception on your part. The Lord is not finished with you. You are a child of God and a child of life. You have to believe in yourself. Do not depend upon anyone else.

You are filled with fears. There is fear of sickness, fear of dying, fear of loving, fear of growing in the love of God, fear of asking forgiveness, fear of being useless, fear of old age and what to do, fear of being put on a shelf, fear of being a burden to others, and fears of all types.

All of these things are really happening to you. Life is changing and it never will be the same again. What has happened in the past is over. It does not mean that life is ended. It could mean that the future will be better. Just when you suspect that you are useless, the Lord could call you to something greater. The Lord is never finished with you. There is a great quote from Yogi Berra, "It is not over, till it's over." The same is true of life. You are in the hands of the Lord and He does not like to lose. So hang in there.

Fears of all kinds slow you up in the love and service of the Lord. Remember the young man who asked the Lord, "What more must I do?" The Lord told him to sell and give to the poor. The young man turned away sad. You are afraid to share your faith, afraid to share your religious experience, afraid to open your hearts to the new, afraid of making a fool of yourself for the Lord, afraid to change in any way. All of these fears and others block your relationship to the Lord. Fears hurt you and do violence to your spiritual life.

There is a tremendous fear of dying. People fear the future life. The only ones who are afraid of dying are those who have not really lived life to the fullest. There is no fear of dying if you have really enjoyed life. If you have lived every day in the presence of God, the fear of dying is less powerful.

Confused	Confounded	Dazed	Disconnected
Disoriented	Frustrated	Puzzled	Wondering
Dubious	Floundering	Flustered	Frantic

Frequently things happen in the course of a day which affect you. It is good to know the feelings. It will help you in understanding the situation and your own reactions. Remember that feelings are neither right nor wrong. You should know them, to understand yourself and God's love of you.

✝ **For your reflection:** *Grace builds on nature. The more you know about yourself, the more you can rid yourself of things which block your intimacy in loving God. What are your fears? Perfect love casts out all fear.*

47. **Fear of Dying**

Another fear which hinders your growth in the love of God is the fear of dying. You are afraid of death. You are afraid for yourself and you are afraid for others whom you love.

Before my mother passed away, I belonged to a prayer group. Whenever we met, I repeatedly related to them, the sick condition of my mother. We prayed. Finally, one of the ladies came up to me after the meeting and said, "Father, you will find no peace within yourself until you give your mother to the Lord." I was shocked and wondered how could a person say that to me. I loved my mother very deeply. It took me almost a year to really give into those words. I finally said to the Lord, "My mother is in your hands and I cannot do much about holding on to her. She is also your child." Peace just filled me.

It is true. You are all in the hands of the Lord. There is nothing you can do about clinging to another person. You are all in the hands of the Lord. Your hands are tied.

I had also imagined what it would be like at her death bed. I tried to think of the prayers that I would say. I imagined how I would feel after she passed away.

Do you know, that all the things that I had imagined and thought about never materialized? The Lord came and took her and carried me along with His graces.

You know that you are dying every day. Every second draws you closer to your departure from this earth. You die every day to self. You die a bit when you sacrifice for others. You die to self when you fight against your temptations. As you die to self, you are being purified like gold in a furnace. You become more beautiful.

All of these things need to take place for you to enjoy the resurrection. When the moth dies it becomes a butterfly. When Jesus died, there was the resurrection. When you die, there is your resurrection.

Strictly speaking you do not die. You never die. The body dies, your works die, but you do not die. You go on to eternal life. Death is like turning over in your sleep. You turn from human life, to experiencing divine life.

I do have some regrets. My mother wanted to tell me about her death. We would be at dinner or sitting in the living room and she would bring up the subject. I always told her I did not want to talk about it. When she died, I never knew what she really wanted. I had to do what I thought she desired. I learned later from others some of the things Mom wanted.

I should have taped her knowledge of the family and its history. She was the last one of her family and all the knowledge went with her. I still regret it.

Learn to live each day. The past is dead and cannot be repeated. Let it go and trust in the Lord. You will be living a life of faith. A day will come in your lives when the separation will take place.

I remember, all too vividly, the last time I had to take Mom to the hospital. When we walked to the door, Mom stopped. She just looked back into the house and her eyes went from room to room. Her eyes and memory took in everything. It was a look that I will never forget. In that moment she gave me an appreciation of her life and sufferings and undertakings to make her family a home. When she finished looking, she turned, and we went outside to the hospital. It was her last visit at home.

Enjoy life. Enjoy each day. Enjoy your loved ones. Do not waste time on bad memories, worries about the future, regrets, and self pity. Learn to trust in God. Let God be God. Do your thing. Your life should be filled with positive thinking. All negative faults must be avoided. Pray as if everything depended on God and work as if everything depended on you. It is a great formula for living a happy and contented life. Try not to worry about today. Try to fulfill some of your greatest desires.

Here are a few more 'feeling' words:

Awful	Blue	Brokenhearted	Dejected
Despairing	Ignorant	Grief-stricken	Lonely
Downcast	Despondent	Woeful	Gloomy
Grim	Heavyhearted	Hopeless	Ignored
Joyless	Imposed upon	Left out	Sorrowful
Low	Melancholy	Mean	Pensive
Miserable	Pessimistic	Rotten	Weepy

Do not play games with life. Stay healthy, eat properly, and get plenty of rest. Pray and develop loving friendships. You do not want to waste your life. There are no second chances and no replays. Your happiness in this life is entirely in your hands. At the end, you cannot blame anybody but yourself. You are your best friend or your worst enemy.

Life is not a dress rehearsal.

✠ **For your reflection:** *How do you face the fact that, one day you will be called by the Lord?*

48. **Death**

The fears of dying and death have a great deal of impact on your way of life. These feelings are real and manifest your degree of faith or lack of faith in the Word of God. Death is a fact which cannot be denied. Sooner or later you have to face your feelings and not keep them hidden. You cannot run away from life. Try to go back in your life and see when these ideas and feelings originated.

It is necessary to understand your feelings in this area of your life and to admit to them. This understanding will help you adjust to the conditions of life. It will also aid you in attempting to explain death to your children or grandchildren. How do you do this?

I remember when I was a child. A person was waked in the home. At an early age, I came face to face with death and the coffin and the wake and so on. I remember waking up one night and my father coming into the room and asking, "Why are you so restless?" I told him, I was afraid to die. In the middle of the night, he said, "Are you afraid that you will wake up, dead?" Strange as it may seem to be, that answer satisfied me. At other times I imagined that if God wanted me, He would hurl down a knife from heaven. I was fast, and I could see myself ducking the hurled knife and escaping out of the room. The Lord would then have to try to send another. In the meantime, I could watch and be prepared.

I have had several events in which I was close to death: Once, in Lake Erie, another, in an automobile accident, thirdly, an operation. The Lord has been good to me. My guardian angels have protected me in many ways. Some I recognized and many were unknown to me, I thank God every day for my guardian angels.

My grandmother taught me to pray for a 'happy death'. I did not understand what she meant. I have done this all my life. However, my fears come to power on different occasions. I just try to live every day in the presence of God. My prayer days start with asking the Lord to bless me. In the evening, I pray that the angels protect me. That is all I can do.

When you understand your feelings of death, you can know and feel for others. Words do not have much meaning at the time of death. Your presence, a hug, a promise of prayers, is the way to meet the situation and give comfort to another.

For children, you cannot give a deep explanation. They haven't any concept of life. For instance, a little boy who was about to lose his two-year-old sister, was in tears. He had always played with her. His mother told him, "Your little sister has been sick for a long time and she was even sick inside of me.

Now, she will have new worlds to play in and will be healthy." This answer satisfied the boy. When you understand your own feelings, it helps you feel for others.

Death is really a love relationship between you and God. The love which keeps you alive here on earth is the same love which gives you life in heaven. St. Paul says that everything else fails and the only thing that remains is love. Jesus said, "In my Father's house, there are many mansions and I will come and take you with Me. Where I am, you also may be." Love does not want to be separate. In life, many of you have experienced, what it means for either one of you to be away. You miss each other. You experience love, in the same way. The only thing that is not lost in death is your love for each other. That relationship remains the same. Be not afraid. Hold the hand of the other. You will be joined in heaven, the same way you are joined on earth. That statement should make you think. Remember that Jesus loves you.

✢ **For your reflection:** *What do you think about the following statement? Your relationship to your spouse, here on earth, is parallel to your relationship to God.*

Sturm family - 1924

49. **Positive Attitudes**

There are many negative feelings, such as prejudice, pride, jealousy, depression, loneliness, pessimism, frustration and many others. When you are not happy then you are contaminated by negative feelings. In order to transform them, there are certain steps to know. First, recognize the feeling and name it. Secondly, do not blame anybody or anything for the feeling. The feeling is in you and it is your feeling. Thirdly, what steps are you going to take to get over the feeling?

As I have been writing, I have jotted many names of feelings. Take a look at them and try to recognize your feeling. Once you identify the feeling and what it is doing to you, you will be able to ignore it, tolerate it or work to get rid of it. In other words, try to understand the feeling and what it does to you.

Feelings are so personal that everyone needs to discover ways and means of accepting, tolerating or freeing yourself of those feelings. I call it, tricks to heal yourself. I have learned to take a ride in the country to rid my fear of anxiety. I have learned that the best method is to understand what the feeling does to me. This frees me of the feeling.

Feelings are like clouds in the sky that come and go. Some are thick and dark, some are fleeting, and some seem to return time and time again. I try to understand the circumstances when certain feelings arise. When I know the circumstances, then I can avoid them. In other words, you have to be aware of yourself and to study your reactions to persons, places and things. You have to learn the tricks of living. That is the reason you should read good books and articles, make a day of recollection, spend time before the Blessed Sacrament, and imitate the sayings and teachings of Jesus. In short, improve your body, mind and heart. You are never too old to learn. You are responsible before the Lord for your gift of life. Jesus had to grow in wisdom, age and grace in the same manner.

Remember the parable when the master gave three different amounts of money to three people. One tripled the amount. One doubled the amount. One buried it in the ground that he would not lose it. The Lord has given you a life and gifts. What have you done or what are you doing to improve? Only you can answer.

When you rise in the morning, even before getting a cup of coffee, what is your attitude? How do you start the day? What will be the tone of your day? How you meet each challenge depends on your attitude. If you rise and say today will be a great day and say a prayer, you have the advantage in the struggles of life. However if you rise in a bad mood and say no prayer, do not blame the Lord or anyone else for your moods. Your feelings are all self made and do not come from anyone else or any other circumstance.

Developing positive attitudes about life is the best way to enjoy life under any circumstances. If you have negative attitudes about life and circumstances, you will never be happy. You will always suffer. You will always be the loser. Some people just enjoy kicking themselves day after day. Some people seem to get enjoyment out of criticizing others. Their enjoyment comes from hurting others. Their negative attitudes govern their way of life.

Develop positive attitudes. The world is full of sorrow, tragedy, war, treason, greed, and power. The world is that way. There is not much that an individual can accomplish to make things right or better. You have to understand this and come to grips within yourself. Pray for the world and the people. Enjoy life as much as you can. Remember the parable when the farmer planted good seed in the field. MT. 13:31. The workmen reported that there were many weeds. The workers desired to go out and pull up the weeds. In 13:28 the Master answered, "An enemy has done this." His slaves said to him, "Do you want us to go and pull them up?" He replied, "No, if you pull up the weeds you might uproot the wheat along with them. Let them grow together until harvest."

That is true of the world. The good and the evil exist together. All you can do is to watch and observe and understand and pray. Do not worry or fret. "All is well." Julian of Norwich, the great mystic, made "All is well," her favorite saying. You should make it your own.

It is not easy to maintain a positive attitude. The world, the news, the television, newspapers, magazines, loss of friends, poverty, and many other events have a negative impact on your lives. For events that are not under your control, you have to allow God to handle the situations. In addition, there are family situations, young people living together, and many other disturbances. You cannot carry the burdens of the world on your shoulders. The only thing, which is in your total control, is you. Trust in the Lord for the rest. Just remember that Jesus loves you and forgives you. That thought is the best positive attitude.

✦ **For your reflection:** *Can you begin each day with a positive attitude and a prayer?*

50. **Discernment**

Feelings are either positive or negative. They are movements in the soul, the positive that they may be accepted, and the negative that they may be rejected. The feelings are neither right nor wrong. It is your task to be able to discern how the Holy Spirit is working in you. The general principles in guiding you are, never make a serious decision, when you are on top of the world (called consolation) and never make a serious decision when you are in deep sorrow or despair (called desolation). When you are in consolation, everything appears peaceful and beautiful. You should never make a decision in these times, for it does not prepare you for future difficulties. You should not make a serious decision when you are in desolation for you have lost the value of things and life. When you are overcome by passions, you are not free to make a decision. Consider what happens when sexual feelings get the better of you.

Signs of consolation times are: when the soul is aroused by the Holy Spirit to a deeper love of the Lord for all things, when you are moved to tears for sorrow for sin, or the sufferings of Christ or His people, when you have increased in faith, hope or love.

Signs of desolation are: darkness of the soul, turmoil in the mind, restlessness due to many temptations, a loss of love and a feeling of being separated from God. You are lost and afraid and full of anxiety and guilt.

In the time of grief, life is empty. You are in desolation. Nothing has any value. The glitter of life has gone dark. You decide to give up your home and live with the children, you decide to give up the car to a grandchild, you feel as if life has ended and what is the use of living. You give up anything that has great value. What good are all those things if you do not have your loved one? When you are deep in grief, let things remain the same for at least a year. By the end of the year, you have met reality alone and will know what you need or do not need. If you jump to decisions too quickly, you will always regret making any of the above judgments.

I was in the Society when my dad died. Shortly after, my mother wrote and told me that she was going to sell her home. The plan was to put the money from the house and share buying another home with my brother. He needed a bigger home for his growing family. A room would be built onto the house for my mother. It was a beautiful brick house in Lancaster. I immediately called and wrote and said, "Please do not go ahead with your plans." I called a priest in Buffalo and told him to persuade my mother not to sell. Thanks be to God she changed her plans, went out and got a job at Worthington Steel. She retired with a good pension and health plan. This was a real blessing of God. When it is at all possible, never live with your children. All privacy is lost for both families. Trust in the love and care of the Lord.

The same thing is true in consolation. In times of consolation never make a change. Stand firm in the way of life, which has guided you up to the present time. The feelings are so powerful that they drown out good judgment and clear reasoning. The consolation hinders you from perceiving possible dangers and difficulties in the future. You cannot be blinded by passion, and come to a reasonable decision.

In attempting to make a serious decision or commitment, there are certain rules to be adapted.

1. What are the pros and cons of the situation?
2. Listen to really unbiased opinions.
3. If you make a decision, what will you be doing five years from now? Can you live peacefully with the decision?
4. Pray and get others to pray
5. Make the decision.

One of the effects of original sin is that you do not understand your feelings. Too often the feelings sway judgments and then there is difficulty. Look at what sexual feelings can do to you? The same is true for all feelings, positive or negative. Do not allow feelings to overcome you. Feelings are wonderful in their beauty but difficult to control. That is why you need prayer and grace of God, for good discernment. Common sense is the best guide.

✠ **For your reflection:** *Do you desire to live a life dependent on your family or be independent and self-sufficient?*

51. Daily Discernment

In order to discern the will of God every day, it is necessary to pray and test the spirits. That is what you are told in the Scripture. It really is common sense. There are times when you find it difficult to discern what is God's will in the present circumstances. Frequently I have a day planned. In the course of the day the phone rings and I am asked to do something. Now what do I do when I have two engagements at the same time? Sometimes they can be resolved and other times you have to pray and use your common sense. When you make this decision, you have to trust that you are doing the right thing and it is according to the will of God. Later on in life, you may look back and see it was a mistake. However, at the time you believed you were doing the right thing. In the sight of God it has not changed. It was the right thing for you. Now when you look back and understand it was a sinful act, does not make it sinful. You cannot change the past. It remains the same. The rule to remember is this: Do not judge a past act on present knowledge,

The older you become, the more you begin to look back over your life. This is a bad practice. You are looking back on the things you did or did not perform and you are using present knowledge. It is impossible to review the past in minute detail. You are only trying to punish yourselves for the way you were. Please do not go through that process. Let the past be as it is. It will not get better by pursuing it. Jesus said, "Let the dead bury the dead." The past is dead. Enjoy life and do not fret or worry about the past. St Basil said, "Only chose what you like, use your intuition so as not to weary the Spirit and lose valuable time in your life." Remember, do not judge a past act on present knowledge.

When you analyze your day, you will find that you make many decisions. If you have made any mistakes, you can try to correct them. You see their effects instantly. Then again you may have made a decision and even prayed about it. You sincerely believed you were doing the right thing. Later on in life you discover the error. Guilt may settle in or guilt will hit you later on in life. There is nothing you can do about it to correct it. You can go to confession and admit your guilt. With the Lord all is forgiven. The difficulty is that you cannot forgive yourself. The mercy and love of God have forgiven you. Now begin to live the life of faith. Forgive yourself.

I will give you a little example. My father taught piano lessons. He desired to teach me and did for two years. I decided that I did not want to learn. I gave my mother a hard time because I did not practice or reluctantly went through the motions. My aunt told me that someday you will regret not being able to play. As I look back, one of the things I regret in life is that I cannot play the piano. I cannot ask forgiveness of my mother or my dad. I have to forgive myself. I regret it. At the time, I thought that I was right because I wanted to play sports.

The major difficulty in all of this is you grow older and wiser as the days go on. When you look back, it is very difficult to relive those moments. Consequently, it is impossible to make a judgment on your decision at that time. The general principle to practice is this. YOU NEVER JUDGE A PAST ACT ON PRESENT KNOWLEDGE. The past cannot be improved; it will not change because you have a deeper understanding of life.

You cannot make it into a sin today.

Do not punish yourself for what you did years ago. When you acted in those days, you believed that you were doing right. Sometimes you may have sinned and confessed it or maybe you don't remember. In any case, the sin is forgiven and you need to trust in the mercy of God. In God's sight you were fine. You have to learn to forgive yourself. Remember that you are never to judge a past act on present knowledge. Jesus always forgives you. His mercy is like a wild fire. It cannot be put out. It cannot be quenched.

The safest rule to follow in life is: pray and use common sense. In this way, you can be certain for your sake, and your later life will be guilt free. Use the advice of St. Basil: St Basil said, "Only choose what you like, use your intuition so as not to weary the Spirit and lose valuable time in your life."

In the course of a day there are many choices. If you pray and use common sense and believe you are doing right, that is the will of God for you. Some people feel unloved. Some people may feel forgotten but that is their problem and not your problem. The principal of life is to help those you can help. Then there are circumstances where you have other choices. When you decide to act, if another blames you for not helping them, you need not ask forgiveness or explain your answer. You believed that you were doing right.

Never worry about doing the will of God. He loves you so much that no matter what you do, He just loves you. He may not fully enjoy what you are doing, but He still loves you. However, if you pray and try to lead a good life, you will be doing God's will. Never fear.

✟ **For your reflection:** *How do you handle the many decisions in the course of the day?*

52. Divine Mercy

People have the mistaken idea that they are able to work and pray their way into Heaven. It is important to know that it is only through the mercy of God that you are saved. St. Paul tells us in Titus 3:15, God saved us, "not because of any righteous deeds we had done, but because of His mercy. He saved us by the baptism of rebirth and renewal of the Holy Spirit."

The mercy of the Lord is important because it is the indispensable key to many earthy blessings, including the blessing of peace.

It is also important to remind yourselves and others of the words of St.

Paul. In the letter to the Hebrew's 4:16 it says, "let us confidently approach the throne of grace to receive mercy and favor and to find help in time of need." Consequently you have the sacrament of penance and the Eucharist. The Fathers of the church used to say that the best attribute of God was His mercy and kindness.

You go through life and commit many sins, transgressions, pains and hurting your neighbors. There are sins of the flesh, breaking the vow of fidelity, and many others. Frequently the same sin is repeated time and time again. It gets so, that looking on your life and seeing the goodness of God, it is very difficult to understand how He could forgive you? In fact when you look at the atrocities of leaders of countries, the abortionists, you do not want to pray for them. How can God forgive them? However, they are all part of His family. They are children of God. I also pray for the mercy of God upon the abortionists.

Never doubt the mercy of God in any circumstance. For instance, when the woman was caught in adultery and brought to Jesus, He said in John 8:10. " Woman where are they? Has no one condemned you?" She replied, "No one sir." Then Jesus said, "Neither do I condemn you, and from now on do not sin any more." He did not give her a punishment. Her sins were many. Jesus appeared to the Disciples after they had deserted Him and His first words were, "Peace be to you." There was not one word of condemnation. Then He showed them His hands and side. Do you think that Jesus suffered for only a few? He died for all His children. He died for you personally.

When you love someone you are willing to forgive them. Take the example of your own family. How often did the children disobey and you loved them? You tried to show your family how much you loved them. If you do that for your children, do you think that you are better than God? We are all God's children. He loves each one. You are a special child.

Consider the sufferings of parents whose children are on drugs or have AIDS. They love their children and desire them to be at peace. They sacrifice a great deal of their lives for the children. Jesus sacrificed His life for the children of God. The sacrifice is not to go in vain. Jesus died for all.

It is never too late to ask for mercy. The thief on the cross, after a life of crime, recognized his failures, and turned to Jesus and said, "Jesus, remember me when you come into your kingdom." Jesus replied, "Amen, I say to you this day you will be with me in paradise." Never give up hope for anyone. Everyone is a child of God. Everyone is in the loving hands of the Lord. He does not desire to lose anyone. Trust in His love and mercy. My Mother used to pray to the good thief. She would say, I know he is in heaven and he certainly is not too busy. Who prays to the good thief?

No matter what is your record, Jesus will forgive you. This is necessary to realize. Jesus does not live in the past. You remember the past and the things you did wrong. For Jesus that is not part of His love, to remember the past and bring it up to you. When you love someone, the object is to forgive and to forget. You never bring up the past to put another down or take advantage of him. As far as the love of Jesus is concerned, He does not remember. He does not keep books.

You are shown mercy in confession. With the feeling of being wiped clean, you should show mercy to others. Manifest kindness, compassion and mercy to all. Jesus had compassion on the multitude. Have faith in the word of God. He loves you and forgives you. Never give up hope.

The Sacrament of Penance is Jesus' Easter gift to you. Your heart should be filled with gratitude. Jesus knew that you were weak and would need healing. Thus, He gives you this sacrament of Mercy. It would be a wonderful sign of your love if you invited someone back to confession. Bring him in yourself. You would be a marvelous example for manifesting the mercy of the Lord. Pray over it. Jesus loves you and the neat part is, He always forgives you.

✠ **For your reflection:** *His mercy is His best attribute.*

Fr. John and his Father. Canisius High School Graduation - 1935

53. **Peace**

The Lord has given you the gift of peace. Jesus said to His Disciples, "My Peace I give to you, my Peace I leave with you." John 14-27. You have the gift of peace. You are made in the image and likeness of God. You posses all the spiritual gifts. If you do not feel them, pray that the Holy Spirit opens your heart and eyes to uncover them. You have not found the pearl of great price. You have not discovered them or opened yourself to them. The reason you have the gift of life is to discover your own beauty and gifts and then share them with your neighbor. Imagine how easy life would be if your neighbor was at peace with you and the world? How great you would feel if you lived in the peace of Christ.

The Lord has not only given you the gift of peace but He also has given you means and ways of discovering it in yourself and means to protect it once discovered. You can always ask the Lord to forgive you. He has given you the Sacrament of Reconciliation. He has given you the pearl of great price. It is a Sacrament of rejoicing. It is a Sacrament of freeing up the spirit within you. It is a Sacrament of belonging. You belong to Christ.

Have you ever thought about the opening prayer of confession? BLESS ME FATHER, FOR I HAVE SINNED.

You ask the Lord to bless you not because you have done something good but because YOU HAVE SINNED. Imagine approaching someone for a loan whom you have just ridiculed in his presence? Imagine going to the bank and defaulting on many payments and asking for a loan? I know what my dad would have said if I had not brought the car back on time. It would be needless to ask for the car again until I was more true to my word.

But you can go to the Lord and ask Him to bless you and to forgive you. You not only ask to be forgiven but you want the Lord to bless you. The amazing mercy of God does exactly as you request. He blesses you and forgives you that you regain the gift. You leave filled with new hope and new life and peace. You are His child. You should leave rejoicing as the shepherds did when they saw and felt the warmth of the love of Jesus.

When you go to confession, say something nice you accomplished during the week. Do not dwell on the negative. You really have to begin thinking positively about yourself no matter what you have done. Positive thinking helps to conquer temptations. As soon as you say I cannot help myself, you are already lost. You are negative and not at peace. Try it. Try it. Try.

Practice positive thoughts about yourself and add a good deed to your confessions, in addition to your sins. Confessions will not become a bore. It is a sacrament of rejoicing. You are reconciled with God, your neighbor and yourself. What more do you desire? Many people go face-to-face in the confessional. I find it faith filled and comfortable. It adds newness and the sense that the priest hears you and understands you. It is like talking to a friend rather than a stranger. Both methods are open to you for your devotion. Reconciliation is a Sacrament of JOY. Remember Jesus loves you and the neat part is, He always forgives you.

✢ **For your reflection:** *Think about the phrase, "Bless me, Father, for I have sinned." What does it do to you? Do you have the feeling of Joy?*

54. **Sacrament of the Eucharist**

Another Sacrament of Joy is the Eucharist. Jesus came, not only to manifest His Love, but He also set up the means to grow in that love. He really did not leave you orphans. He presented you with His Body and Blood to nourish and protect you. Just as you need food and drink to survive, so you need the spiritual strength and the grace of God to live. You receive the real Body and Blood of Jesus under the sign of bread and wine. It is not a symbol. It is the real thing.

The host and the wine remain the same on the outside but the substance of the bread and wine become the Body and Blood of Jesus. The theological word is transubstantiation. That is your faith. It is not a symbol.

Pope John Paul says about the Eucharist, "It is the source and summit of a Christian life." It is the source of strength to live and conquer temptations and to grow in love. You carry within you, the Body and Blood of Jesus similar to the way Jesus is present in the monstrance. You are really a temple of God. Keep the temple sinless. Sin of all sorts takes away the full effect of the Eucharist. You can still face the trials and sufferings of life bravely. Jesus comes to you as a best friend. He sees your heart open and He can fill you with peace and forgiveness and healing. He will not force Himself on you. He is your personal friend.

The Eucharist is both a meal and a sacrifice. The Lord gave you the Eucharist at the Last Supper because He desired you to realize that He loves you. You become united to God in Baptism, Penance and Confirmation, but the Eucharist nourishes you daily. You become more like Christ. Jesus says, "Whoever eats my flesh and drinks my blood remains in me and I in him." John 6:56

It is a meal of friendship and unity and also a sacrifice. Jesus died for your sins, to conquer death and enter the Kingdom of Heaven. Jesus came to reunite you to the love of the Father. It is a meal of rejoicing. Jesus conquered sin and death. You are now children of God and belong to His family. When you go to communion, do you ever think about the prayer which everyone says: "Lord, I am not worthy to receive you, but only say the word and I WILL BE HEALED." Do you really believe those words? Did you ever feel any healing within you? Do you give time for the Lord to speak to you after you receive? Is it merely eat and run which is a favorite pastime of Americans? There are some who follow that pattern in church. It is a great sign of faith to give proper time to God.

It is a meal of rejoicing. I have been to weddings and around the table of people who are laughing, talking and having a good time. People eat a piece of wedding cake with a smile on their faces. I have been around a long time and the longest faces are in churches. Do you think that Jesus went around with a long face at the wedding feast? Looking solemn does not give you any more graces than if everyone had a smile on their face. "Rejoice in the Lord always, again I say rejoice." Phil. 4-4. Jesus knows you by name.

I like Charlie Brown; no matter how he feels, he comes up smiling and with a positive attitude. Many have serious problems and the Lord knows them all. You are in His hands. He does not desire you to carry the troubles of the world upon your shoulders. He wants you to be happy and at peace. Keep thinking positively. There is a great song from years ago which says much about life. "Let a smile be your umbrella on a rainy, rainy day. And if your sweetie cries just tell her that a smile will always pay." A smile attracts a smile and your troubles are lighter. The world is in God's hands and not yours. Trust in the Lord. Give your problems to the Lord in the Eucharist. Attitude does much in problem solving. Prayer does not hurt but heals. It is the answer.

When you receive the Body and Blood of Jesus, you are sharing a Divine meal. Pray silently in your hearts and share with the Lord your thanks and ask Him to help you through the day. When you go to a banquet you do not leave immediately and say good-bye but you linger with the people. Do not short change Jesus and eat and leave. It is an insult to the Lord. It is not good deportment and it gives a bad example. Stay and share time with the Lord. This is a most intimate time. Jesus is within you. You carry Him close to your heart. He desires to share with you His love and you can allow your heart to speak to His Heart. Be jealous for the intimacy of the moment. It is like having a lover holding you tenderly and lovingly. Jesus is delighted being with you.

You recall the scene in the Garden of Olives, when Jesus was suffering? He asked the Disciples to pray. After a short time, He returned and found them sleeping. He said, "Can't you watch one hour with me?" MT. 26-40. The same is true today. It is disheartening to see people leave the church early and rush out.

✠ **For your reflection:** *Lord, I am not worthy to receive you but only say the word and I will be healed.*

55. Bad Things vs. Good People

Life is a journey and not a guided tour. The Lord does guide you but only the way you desire to go. You have a free will. He does not determine the way for you. Jesus is the way but you do not know how to read the map. There are many signs and helps but you do not take the time to stop and get the directions. It is much like trying to put a toy together. Many people attempt to put it together and when they fail, they finally read the instructions. The same is true in life. You go along every day and seem to be in total control. Then some crisis hits and finally you may turn to God in prayer. You pray earnestly. Does it take a crisis to wake you up, that there is a God who loves you? You cry out, "Why me?"

Life is like a river. It does not stop or wait and it cares not what it carries and just moves along. There is no explanation of life. It is a total mystery. It is not a mystery for God. Life is like a woven picture. God sees the front of the beautiful tapestry, which is the reality of life. You see the back, the knots and twirls and cutoffs. All you can do is swim in the river to the best of your ability. If you are caught in a crisis, cancer, death and other disabilities, all you can do is to try to accept it. There is no use blaming God. He had nothing to do with it. Human nature builds the quilt and human nature is to blame. You are today what has been handed down to you.

Do not waste time blaming God. It will do no good. You will only get worse. Pray to think on a positive note and appreciate what you can accomplish.

The only thing that is important is, today, the present moment. You cannot improve the past. No matter what you do or think, you cannot improve the past. Try to live in the present and pray. God is really on your side. He knows what it is to suffer. The Blessed Mother is a great example and model of suffering.

You often say "WHY ME?" I cannot give you any reason but Jesus did cry out in the garden to His Father, "Let this cup pass from me, yet, not my will but your will be done." When bad things happen there is no answer. It is a mystery and in a way it is the beautiful mystery of your faith. The Lord Jesus said you need to take up your cross daily and follow Him. If He had to suffer, why should you be excused? Even the Blessed Mother was not excused and she was sinless. God did not spare His own Son from pain.

There is no answer to the question, why me? It is really a part of your life. You have one thing. I have another. There is no use comparing because that does not heal the situation in the least. It only aggravates the wound. Give the crisis to the Lord and put it at the foot of the cross. Add it to the pains of Jesus for the sins and sickness of the world. You will be blest like the thief on the cross.

It is a strange irony of life that the rich get richer. Others are more blest than you. All good things happen to them and nothing good happens for you. I do not know the answer. However, I do know that it is not worthwhile complaining. You only get more angry and filled with a critical spirit. You are only wasting time and not enjoying life. There is no need to allow others or crisis to stop you from enjoying life to the best of your ability. God knows the answer to all things. Try to go along with God. He knows and understands your difficulties. He blesses and rewards you for the effort of remaining faithful. Your suffering is never in vain.

Even if you have been a good churchgoing person, bad things may happen to you. Look at the Blessed Mother. Circumstances may seem bad for you, but in the sight of God, good will be done as time goes on. In the long run, what makes you believe that it was bad in the first place? Rom. 8:28 "We know that all things work for good for those who love God, who are called according to his purpose." You just may not see it. You are part of the beautiful tapestry of life. Look at Job in the Old Testament. He had everything and then became afflicted. It took him some time to reconcile it with the Lord but He finally gave in. The same will be true of you. Once you surrender to God and do not demand your own will, peace will reign in your heart. No matter what the crisis, or the rough road, or the hurts, remember the face of Jesus as He suffered for you on the cross.

✠ **For your reflection:** *In your troubles recall the face of Jesus.*

56. **Communication and Prayer**

In life you know that communication is necessary. Communication of its nature demands that one listens while the other talks. Prayer has the same two dimensions, while you pray, Jesus listens. In real communication and prayer, you have to listen as Jesus talks.

Listening is an art. How do you listen? Do you use one or two ears? Are you like the old couple who just celebrated their 60th anniversary? As they sat in the porch, he said, "I love you." She said, "Speak a little louder you know that I am deaf." He repeated, " I love you." She said, "I am tired of you too."

Is your attitude such that your heart is open to another? Or is your heart closed? Jesus told the people, "He who has ears to hear let him hear." LK. 14-35 It seems that hearing and listening depends on the attitude of the person. You may find in your experience of life that you listen to one who loves you as you listen to God in prayer

Your spiritual life and natural life probably follow the same pattern. Do you remember the story of the farmer who was sowing seeds in the fields? Some fell on rocky soil, some fell in the thickets, some fell on the path, and some fell on good soil. You listen to God and each other in the same way.

You can listen in such a way that it goes in one ear and out the other. You really do not care one bit about what is being said. For instance how do you listen to the gospel on Sunday? Does it make any difference for you, or in you? You probably listen to others in the same way.

There are three major ways of listening. The first is called rejection. You just do not pay attention to the other.

The second is toleration. You can listen with one ear and forget. Then again you may think if I was in that situation I would feel the same. Or, you may be more tolerant and say you understand, and you do what you can.

The third major way of listening is the best. It is called acceptance. Here you listen with all your heart and mind and body. You really desire to be a necessary part of the other person and God. Here you accept the other person entirely.

Communication in life is the same as communication in prayer. You may be stubborn and do not want to change. You may just be in the mood not to listen. Whatever is said is really not important enough for you. You may have the attitude of getting even. Namely, that you were not heard and now you are not going to listen. You may believe you are too tired to give the time to listen. You may think I have heard all your ramblings before, so it really is not important to me. These reasons and many more excuses interfere with communication and prayer. Examine yourselves. I cannot do it for you. Two of the marvelous components of communication and prayer are TRUST and HONESTY.

Examine how you attend Mass and listen to the readings. Do you give any extra time to God or only what is necessary? Is that really love? Do you treat your family in the same way? Do you ever ask for forgiveness of each other? How about God in the Sacrament of Penance? Love is hard work and it takes effort as you well know and all is not a bed of roses. The love of God and prayer are the same. There are ups and downs. However, you always have to put in the effort. My mother used to say when she could no longer get to Mass, "John, I am glad that I lived the way I did for now I can no longer do anything, I have few regrets."

Life is short. Use your gift of life to share the proper time with each other, your work and God. Communicate and pray. He always forgives you.

> *It is not by your money*
> *But by your capacity to love,*
> *That you are rich or poor.*
> *To strive for wealth*
> *And have no capacity to love,*
> *Is to be like the bald man,*
> *Who struggles to collect combs.*
>
> *—Anonymous*

✟ **For your reflection:** *How do you evaluate yourself as a listener? How do you listen to God? How do you listen to your spouse, family? How do you listen to your neighbor, stranger? Remember, you are all children of God.*

57. **Life is a Gamble**

The word 'temple' in Hebrew means, the dwelling place of Yahweh. In the scriptures you are called temples of the Holy Spirit. Temples were the most ornate buildings. The Temple at the time of Jesus, actually the Third Temple built by Israel, was indeed magnificent, "like a snowy mountain glittering in the sun," said Josephus, the first century historian. The Temple was built of three different shades of marble and overlaid with so much gold that it could not be looked at in the midday sun, on account of its brightness. The interior had the most precious wood of olive and cedar. Tables and ornaments were made of the purest gold and covered with diamonds and precious stones. This is the Temple of which all that presently remains is the Western or Wailing Wall, a remnant of the Temple Mount enclosure with stones, some of them, that weigh over 100 tons.

You are described as a temple beautiful beyond all comparison, more beautiful than any ornate temple. You and your body are monuments of beauty in the sight of God. You are so beautiful that God cannot stop loving you. 1 Cor. 3-16 "Do you know that you are the temple of God and the Holy Spirit dwells within you? All the Lord wishes you to do is to enjoy your life. The reason you are born and brought into this world is to enhance its beauty and not to mar it. The more you sense your own worthiness and charms the more beauty you bring to your family and friends and neighbors. You have a purpose.

This book has attempted to share ideas with you to set you free. It is like buying a new car and taking you for a spin. It gives you the opportunity to open your eyes to another spiritual world. You can settle back and do nothing or else give you thought and self confidence to reach out and risk.

Life is really for gamblers. You gamble on your life span. You gamble with the difficulties and trials and happiness of life and love. Sometimes you win and sometimes you lose. However when you gamble to win in the spiritual life, you will never be a loser but always a winner. The winning formula is to love. Live each day for love. Love is the only thing that will not be lost. Everything else will turn to dust and ashes. If you love, you will be the winner.

There is the story of the old miser who loved money and obtained a tremendous fortune. He intended to invest it wisely and then enjoy life in his old age. At that moment an angel appeared to him. It was the angel of death and pointed his finger at him and said, "Come." The man begged and pleaded and got down on his hands and knees and said, "Give me three days more and I will give you half of my earnings." The angel shook his head and would not hear of it. The miser said, " Just give me one more day and I will give you everything I own." The angel began to tug at him.

Finally he was able to get a few moments more to write a note. "You who read this note, if you have enough to live on, don't waste your time accumulating wealth and any other useless thing as honors and prestige. LIVE! All my money could not buy me one single hour of life!" The Lord was not kidding when He said, "Every hair on your head is counted."

My mother had the best philosophy or formula, she said, "I live each day so that I have as few regrets as possible at the end of the day." Another of her sayings,

"If you are going to send me roses send them now that I may enjoy them."

Unwrap your own beauty. Derive your own formulas. Make life worth living. See how great and marvelous the Lord has made you. Everyone is beautiful in the eyes of God. Believe in yourself. There is nothing of which to be ashamed. It is your life. Do not allow the world or others or peer pressure to tell you how to seek happiness. Seek happiness and peace that is within you and not outside of you. You can never be a loser for Jesus loves you and the neat part is He always forgives you.

The following is a special formula:

- You better slow down
- Don't dance so fast
- Life is short
- The music won't last.

Render to Caesar the things that are Caesar's. Render to God the things that are God's. In other words keep your priorities in the right order, love, pray, work, exercise. You are worth it.

✠ **For your reflection:** *How do you face a new day?*

Straight down the middle

58. **Living Life Today**

Lose your mind and find your senses. You all know and realize that life today is a rat race. There is no time for anything. You are accustomed to fast foods, cell phones while eating, two to three cars per family, lines of eight items or less, rush on a vacation, pick up children, and drive them around. There is little family life. It is all go, go, go.

It is about time that you came to your senses and took time for yourselves. Use your common sense.

You deserve nourishing food, not only for the body but also for the soul. Take time out to read a good book, take a walk in the park, visit gardens and smell the flowers, sit and relax and enjoy a good conversation. Take time once a week for yourselves. You deserve it. People get married to love each other. Instead of loving each other you take all the time for the children and outside activities and work. Are those the reasons you were married? I hope not. I can get so involved with priestly work and it is all good, that I forget to take care of myself. I have to stop and play golf. The priests get burnt out if they are not careful. The same applies to you. Love wears out if you really do not share and take time for each other. You wake up one morning and wonder what has happened to me? To us? It is like rust eating away at the car.

You can get so busy and so involved, that you lose your capacity to enjoy life. Then you wonder why life is so boring at home. I have seen beautiful homes with many CD's but I have never heard the music. There are libraries filled with books and I wonder how much time is taken to read? All I hear is, there is no time. You are so busy taking care of your home, and you say there is no time. There is no time.

You should try to enjoy the very simple pleasures of life. Did you ever notice how your cat rests after eating? Did you ever see an animal eat what is not good for them? They follow the laws of nature. Humans just charge on and eat and drink and work and never enjoy. They are a sad group. Life is so short and it is wasted on foolish things and poor use of time. Take time out for each other and time for God. Life is a dance. God danced creation. Get into the dance. Do not sit on the sidelines. Theaters have dress rehearsals to work out the wrinkles. Life is not a dress rehearsal. This is your life, now, today. Use your imagination and take time for each other and for life.

There was an article in the paper recently which stated the Americans were overweight and out of shape. You see very few people walking or riding a bike. The young have all sorts of wheels to get them some place very quickly and then they do not know what to do. Life gets boring. Why waste your body? Keep it healthy, it is the only one you possess.

I wrote these articles that you could discover your own beauty. You have been made from clay but you do the molding.

The Lord challenges you to enjoy His gift of life and the beauty of creation. Women spend hours trying to maintain their beauty. However, you do not spend hours trying to enjoy life. Come to your senses. Stop and smell the roses. Listen to the sound of a bird, the rustle of the wind in the trees. Enjoy the color of a sunset. Enjoy the color changes in the fall. Enjoy. Take time. Did you ever watch the stars at night? Take dancing lessons.

God gave you the beautiful gift of life. Do not waste it on things that will pass. Time is short enough and the older you get the faster it goes. Do things you never did before and wish you had. Take a cruise, go to a baseball game, visit the Rockies, watch the great wonder of the world, Niagara Falls. There is so much beauty to enjoy and it all goes to waste. What a pity. God gave you a beautiful gift so use it. Jesus gives you the gift for which He paid with His life. He loves you and the neat part of it all, He forgives you.

> Life is not a dress rehearsal.
> Dance the dance of life.
> You only go around once.

✠ **For your reflection:** *Have you talked with anyone about how this book has affected your life? Share the good news with others.*

59. **Eucharistic Adoration**

St. Michael's has adoration of the Blessed Sacrament every day. It begins after the morning Masses at 8:00 AM and continues all day till 5:00 PM. You are most welcome to attend. In fact, every morning from 9:00 until 10:30 there are only a few present. I attend every morning. The Lord would appreciate a few more of His children.

We have Niagara Falls within an hour. I very seldom visit, except when visitors come to Buffalo. People travel from all over the world, to see that Wonder. We have a greater Wonder in the Blessed Sacrament. We do not even cross the street or take the time to visit Jesus in the Eucharist. More and more churches are offering Exposition of the Blessed Sacrament. You can find Jesus in every part of the world. Are we not much happier in living at these times, rather than in the time of Jesus? Greater happiness may be found by visiting Christ in the Eucharist. The Lord is slowly inviting all of you to spend some time with Him. It is a great invitation and a wonderful honor to share in the love of Jesus in the beautiful mystery of Love. Right now we all have to pray for the Mercy of God upon us and the world. We are in the Hands of God. We need to come to the aid of each other and the world.

Ought you not feel it a great grace and an honor to be invited by Jesus? You should feel it as a great honor to be in His presence. You should feel it a great delight. Jesus takes delight in your presence. You could pray, "Why is it Jesus that you love me so much? Why are you so delighted in my presence? What have I that so delights you? I have not been living up to your expectations and I have sinned against you. Yet you invite me and love me. All I can do is to try to be grateful for your love of me. Dear Jesus help me to be a good child of yours and never love anyone else."

The following is a passage from the diary of St. Faustina on Eucharistic Adoration concerning visiting the exposition of the Blessed Sacrament, paragraph 1692.

" My Lord and Creator, your goodness encourages me to converse with you. Your mercy abolishes the chasm which separates the Creator from the creature. To converse with You, O Lord, is the delight of my heart. In you I find everything that my heart could desire. Here Your light illumines my mind, enabling me to know you more and more deeply. Here, streams of graces flow down upon my heart. Here my soul draws eternal life, O my Lord and my Creator, You alone, absolve all these gifts, give your own self to me and unite yourself intimately with your miserable creature. Here without searching for words, our hearts understand each other. Here, no one is able to interrupt our conversation. What I talk to you about, Jesus, is our secret. These are secret acts of forgiveness, known only to Jesus and me; this is the mystery of His mercy, which embraces each soul separately. For this incomprehensible forgiveness of yours, I adore you, O Lord and Creator, with all my heart and soul. And although my worship is so little and poor, I am at peace because I know that you know that it is sincere, however inadequate........."

This is a beautiful description of a heart talking to heart.

I think most people do not know what to do when they visit the Blessed Sacrament. People come with books, bibles, litanies, prayers of all sorts, rosaries etc. It is really not wrong but He is the author of all that prayer. There you have in the Blessed Sacrament the Author Himself. Why not share with Him what is in your heart, those things are not written anywhere. It is your secret time with Jesus Himself. People vie for the honor for speaking with the Holy Father alone. Here you can speak with Jesus alone and listen to what He tells you.

To have the opportunity and the grace to be invited to visit Jesus in the

Blessed Sacrament is a rare privilege. Jesus on the other hand is patiently waiting for you to visit with Him. Give Him a full hour of attention. I do not think that you would take a book to see the Pope and then spend an hour reading. Why do it to Jesus?

I was invited to a special dinner for fifty years of marriage. I went and enjoyed the dinner and the company. I did not bring a book, a radio, a cell phone. I spent the time with the couple. It should be the same when you visit Jesus. Here is what I do every day. I first ask the Lord to bless me. Then I give thanks to the angels, Mary, and my favorite saint. I share with Jesus the present burdens. Then I say the chaplet of mercy. All this takes about 12 to 15 minutes. Then I sit in silence and look at the Blessed Sacrament. The seat of the soul is in the heart. I try to sit quietly and concentrate with the attention at the forehead. Try to imagine you are looking straight ahead through your eyes. Remain sitting quietly and you may notice a light appearing or a brightness. This means that your attention is away from your lower body. If you have any distraction say a short prayer as "Jesus, have mercy on me." Outside of those words do not say any prayer. Just try to listen to the Spirit working in you. I try to listen to the Lord with my heart. I frequently close my eyes to get rid of outside distractions. But, all the time I try to be fully attentive to Jesus and I wait patiently for the union of our hearts. This is my time with the Lord. I do not interrupt with my prayers. I just try to listen. I wait for the opportunity to speak "heart to Heart". This is where I can learn more about the Lord and this is where I learn more about His love for me. This is where my spirit is united with the Holy Spirit. This is where I am free from all the stresses and strains of the world. If I am distracted, I say a short prayer " Jesus have mercy on a poor sinner." or "Jesus, I trust in you." or "Jesus I love you."

The time goes quickly, once your concentration is fully placed on Jesus. You need not look at the Blessed Sacrament; you may keep your eyes closed and keep your concentration at the top of your head. Try to look at the area behind your eyes toward the middle of your forehead. This method will take time to learn. You may practice at home by sitting quietly and trying this method for a few minutes every day or frequently.

If your church has adoration try to take time so visit or sign up for a time schedule. How good God is. He makes Himself available to all. How many abuse that love? Sinners of course do not pay attention to the Love of God. Good people too, in their coldness and indifference abuse the love of God. He has been so long with them and still they do not know Him. One day Jesus complained to Sr. Mary Alacoque in a vision when He showed her His

Sacred Heart.

"Behold this heart of mine so full of love for men that it has shed its last drop of blood for them and has given them my own flesh and blood as food and drink for their souls, and consider, how this heart receives from most men in return for so great a love nothing but ingratitude and contempt! But what grieves me most is that I am treated thus even by good and just souls," Taken from "The Blessed Eucharist" by Father Mueller, C.S.S.R.

Your hearts should be touched about such a complaint. You love Him and He loves you. Going before the Blessed Sacrament is a good time to repay Jesus what is due to Him. You can repay Him for all your benefits: benefits of creation, the preservation of the gifts of your life, for the agony in the garden, for the pains of His suffering, and repay Him for His excessive love of you, His forgiveness, His mercy, His love in the Blessed Sacrament. Thank Him for all your very personal gifts.

Love can only be repaid by love. Love is only contented with true love. You return His love in the way you keep the commandments, the love which impels you to receive the Eucharist, the love which encourages you to visit the Blessed Sacrament, the love which motivates you to spend an hour with Him in the Exposition of the Blessed Sacrament. You do not want Jesus to be left alone.

In sharing your love in this manner, you will find that you have more confidence in your prayers. You will also experience the freedom that Jesus has promised. Thus, when the time is ripe Jesus will come and visit you. He will say, "Come, my precious child, because you have been faithful in many things, I will place you over many. Your place has been prepared by Me. Come and see what your eyes have never seen, and your ears have never heard, come and enjoy your Lord forever and ever."

Remember Jesus Loves you and the neat part is He always forgives you.

✟ **For your reflection:** *Take these thoughts with you, as you kneel before the Blessed Sacrament, and see and feel how they will affect your prayer life.*

60. **Mercy vs. Justice**

We have been speaking of love, the love of yourself and the love of God. This love is essential to life and the lives of those around you. We spoke of the necessity of prayer.

The world, including United States, is in a terrible state. You live in dangerous times. Every morning you pick up the newspaper almost dreading the headlines. All of the children of God are fighting, hating, killing and torturing each other. Mothers are killing their children as if they were cattle. Teenagers are committing suicide. Couples live together before they are married. There is extreme poverty in every country. Religious persecution is rampant. Every country and nation is driven by prejudice. The world is in a mess. People want Christ out of Christmas. They desire to have God removed from every song and dance. Prayer is taken out of the schools. There are killings in schools and children are kidnapped. In spite of all this there is coldness and indifference on the part of the political leaders of our country.

Ordinary common sense would say that there is something wrong and let us do something about it. But, NO, we are selfish and greedy and independent and we do not need God in any form whatsoever. Politicians do what they wish, people do not vote, fewer people go to church or pray, youth do not care, indifference is cool, and the country and all the churches have fewer services.

The saving and hopeful picture is there are good people who really pray and sacrifice. For the time being, they keep the world in the merciful hands of God. They do not look for thanks or praise, they believe in the truth of life. The truth is that love is the only lasting and stable element to a peaceful existence and fruitful and neighborly existence. Nothing else will bring peace. It is the only thing which gives the individual peace and it will bring peace to a family and hopefully bring peace to a community and so on. So far in the history of the world not one single war brought peace, forgiveness or healing. In this area common sense goes out the window.

An essential element of love is respect. If you do not respect yourself as a beautiful person, you will never ever be able to respect another person, even your spouse. Doctors who abort babies, lack respect for themselves and the value of human life. Youths who commit suicide do not love themselves or respect themselves. Can't you see how much more beautiful life would be if persons respected themselves, their neighbor, property, God, and could rid themselves of prejudice?

My father taught me respect in many different ways. I remember my dad; he had a special nickname for my mother. One day as I was leaving for school, I was only in second grade, I turned and said good-bye "Kit." Dad was home and heard it. When I returned from school that day, he called me aside and said "You never say that again, she is my wife and she is your mother, so you call her Mom or Mommy but never Kit. I was cured of being fresh.

When I was prefect at Canisius High School, the boys were taught respect. First to respect themselves in the way they dressed and the way they acted and spoke. They were taught to love and respect their parents and their brothers and sisters. In fact I would give them lessons to try at home and I would seek out the results.

They were taught, responsibility. The first lesson was to the incoming freshmen. They were instructed to be on time for school and in the classroom by the first bell. I told them I never ever want you to come to school late and give me the excuse that my mom did not get me up on time. That is the kiss of death. We did not have too much difficulty.

Try this. When you go shopping, hold the door for someone else, nine out of ten times they walk by as if you are the doorperson.

I wonder about the good old days when a man took off his hat in an elevator when a woman was present; when men did not wear hats while eating; I still take off my cap when talking to a lady. Youth do not give preference to the elderly. Try taking a walk. Who gives way on the sidewalk?

The strange part is that we are all children of God, no matter what religion or race or color. God accepts each person as they are. The trouble is that we cannot accept each other. I f God does, why can't we? Consequently, all the bad things mentioned about are the works and the activities of man. God has no part in it and you cannot blame Him.

Right now the world is under the influence of the Mercy of God. The Blessed Mother and Jesus are holding up the arm of God's mercy. If their prayers and our prayers cannot sustain the merciful arm of God, the wrath of God, the arm of justice shall descend. At that point you and the world will be treated as it deserves by what you have done and not done. Pray that the mercy of God prevails and urge others to pray.

No one can predict the future. You need to live each day as it were your last day. The challenge that John the Baptist laid down was, "Reform your lives the Kingdom of God is at hand." Jesus said the same thing when He began His preaching throughout the country. It is still true today. Reform your lives. Pray and get others to pray with you. No one can predict the end time. All I can say is trust in the Word of the Lord and not in the vain promises of others. There are many false prophets.

In the meantime do not fret or get anxious. You and the world are in

God's hands. Enjoy life to the best of your ability. Then you will have no regrets. Do what I believe in, Dance as if no one was watching, Sing as if no one was listening, Enjoy each day with your loved ones and friends. God will take good care of you. What more can you desire? What more do you want? All God asks of you is to pray and love your neighbor. Then all will be well. Julian of Norwich, the marvelous woman mystic, kept repeating, "All will be well, all will be well." She is a Saint. Remember that Jesus loves you and the neat part is He always forgives you. Life is your gift and only goes around once. Enjoy. Life's a Dance and not a dress rehearsal.

For your reflection: *How do you think, after reading this book, your life style will be affected?*

Fr. John & Tim Russert